Public Policy
Toward Labor

Public Policy Toward Labor

ROBERT EVANS, Jr.

Department of Economics
Massachusetts Institute of Technology

Harper & Row, Publishers

NEW YORK, EVANSTON, AND LONDON

Library of Congress Catalog Card Number: 65-13471

Contents

Preface

In the last thirty years the role of the federal government in the field of labor-management relations has grown enormously. As a consequence, it is necessary for the student of labor to have some awareness of the government's current role and how it was developed. The kinds of things which this should include and the degree of detail which should be involved will depend upon the student's ultimate interests. For a number of students the need will be to know and understand the broad perspective of the principal substantive areas of federal policy and to have some appreciation for the historical and contemporary forces which have molded them. This book has been designed for students like these.

In writing this I have attempted to make the subject interesting and alive, suggesting some of the seeming inconsistencies of policies and raising the implications of some of the alternatives. An attempt has been made to avoid the seeming completeness and finality of discussion which seems to characterize so many texts. Ideally, the reader should be left wondering why the author implies this or that and should believe the author to be completely wrong in his evaluation of certain points, for it is only when one critically thinks through a problem for himself that real learning takes place.

I am indebted to a number of people. I am particularly indebted to my colleagues at M.I.T.: Douglass V. Brown, Stanley M. Jacks, Charles A. Myers, and Abraham J. Siegel; students in classes which have covered its subject matter, and to Miss Grace Locke who did the typing with her usual efficiency and pleasantness.

ROBERT EVANS, JR.

Public Policy
Toward Labor

CHAPTER I

The Institutional
Setting

INTRODUCTION

This book is primarily concerned with the development, application, and appropriateness of federal labor policy as it affects union-management relations. Federal labor policy can be divided into two types. One set of policies prescribes the context in which the employee-employer relationship is determined. The second set determines some of the particular conditions of that relationship, such as the minimum wage which may be paid. Due to space limitations and the varied methodology involved in evaluating the different types of policy, it seems appropriate to concentrate on only one set of policies. Thus, the aim of this book is to suggest answers to some policy questions related to the structure within which employer-employee relations are determined. In a sense there has always been a federal labor policy, though for most purposes it is considered to have begun 30 years ago, when, under the leadership of Senator Robert Wagner of New York, Congress enacted its first comprehensive labor statute. This, however, was not the first federal legislation to deal with union organization. That honor belonged to the Erdman Act of 1898 which dealt with the railroads. Nor was it the first federal labor legislation of the early 1930s, for it was preceded by the Norris-LaGuardia Act (1932), Section 7 of the National Industrial Recovery Act (1933), and Public Resolution No. 44 (1934). Yet, because of its far-reaching character and because it contained enforcement provisions, it marked the beginning of a federalized code for employee-employer relations.

In the New Deal Era the Wagner Act was followed by legislation setting up the Social Security system, the federally assisted state unemployment compensation system, and the minimum wage and overtime hours provisions. These latter acts, which governed a portion of the particular substance of the employment relationship, have, in subsequent years, been extended to cover more employees and have had their benefit levels raised. Essentially, however, this legislation has remained unchanged in concept and impact. The same has not been true of the Wagner Act which governed the context within which the relationships between employees, unions, and firms are determined. Basic conceptual changes were incorporated in the Taft-Hartley Act (1947), and in the Landrum-Griffin Act (1959).

Federal legislation as it affects the employment relationship raises a number of difficult and interesting questions. Some of these are:

1. What is federal public policy on specific questions? For example, what can an employer say to his workers? What rights do striking employees have?

2. How is specific policy formed and carried out? Is it only a function of Congress and the courts, or do the parties themselves affect its determination?

3. What are the forces which have shaped policy formation? Why was the Taft-Hartley law passed in 1947 and not before? Is the National Labor Relations Board responsive to the interests of the party whose President is in the White House?

4. In what ways have the behavior and responses of the principal actors (workers, unions, and employers) been affected by these policies? What have these policies meant for the freedom of the individual and the functioning of the economy? If an employer has to bargain with his organized employees, does this really change the resulting conditions of employment?

Answers to these questions are important for an understanding of the American economy and for evaluating proposed changes in federal or state labor legislation. Their discussion will be facilitated by first briefly reviewing: (1) the major provisions of those statutes which form the legal structure; and (2) the methods by which the NLRB operates.

THE NORRIS–LAGUARDIA ACT

The Norris-LaGuardia Act was passed in 1932. Though it contains a provision which makes a "yellow-dog" contract, i.e., a contract which states that the signer will not join a union during the course of his employment unenforceable in the courts, its principal purpose was to limit the issuance of injunctions by federal courts in labor cases. Section 4 of the Act prevents a federal court from issuing a restraining order or an injunction in a case arising out of a labor dispute. A labor dispute is then defined in Section 13 as "any controversy concerning terms or conditions of employment, or concerning the association or representation of persons in negotiating, fixing, maintaining, changing, or seeking to arrange terms or conditions of employment regardless of whether or not the disputants stand in the proximate relation of employer or employee." The principal effect of this last section was to reverse the view held by many federal judges that economic self-help tactics of unions were illegal unless the union members involved were directly employed by the firm being affected. Federal policy thus came to recognize that unionized workers have an economic interest in those conditions which prevail in nonunion segments of their industry as well as those which exist within their own firm.

In many respects the Norris-LaGuardia Act was similar to Section 20 of the Clayton Anti-Trust Act whose provisions had been effectively and severely limited by the U.S. Supreme Court in the early 1920s. The Court had essentially declared that Section 20 contained nothing new, that it only restated the position which the courts had been upholding all along. The Court, in 1938, in *New Negro Alliance* v. *Sanitary Grocery Company*,[1] upheld the constitutionality of the Norris-LaGuardia Act and applied a liberal construction to its meaning. Had the Court been as conservative as it had been earlier, the Norris-LaGuardia Act might have been as impotent as were the labor sections of the Clayton Act. The Court's view of the world has changed and the words "labor dispute" have been interpreted in the broadest possible way.

There are, however, two exceptions to the broad no-injunction command of the Act. One is self-contained; the second arises under the Taft-Hartley Act. An employer, after a hearing in open court before witnesses who have the opportunity to cross-examine, may obtain a temporary restraining order if he is faced with union-induced violence which cannot be controlled by the public authorities. The order will not be granted even then unless the employer makes every effort to settle the dispute, which, according to the Supreme Court, includes a willingness to negotiate, to accept mediation, and to go to arbitration. This combination, plus the procedural safeguards, means that the traditional legal remedies of court orders against violence, intimidation, and other unlawful acts are generally lacking in labor cases. The other allowable type of injunction is in cases where the NLRB seeks an injunction under specific sections of the Taft-Hartley Act. Thus, an employer's chief protection against economic pressure and picket lines by workers who are not his own employees is an injunction obtained by the federal government under provisions of the Taft-Hartley Act. This has meant some diminution in the protection from injunctions which unions originally enjoyed under the Norris-

[1] *New Negro Alliance* v. *Sanitary Grocery Co.*, 303 U.S. 552, 304 U.S. 542 (1938).

LaGuardia Act. In addition, the fact that an administrative agency can obtain judicial relief for an employer not available to him as a private individual raises certain questions concerning the logic of our labor laws.

The Norris-LaGuardia Act does not contain any reference to a removal of unions from the anti-trust laws as set forth in the Sherman and Clayton Acts. It does, however, provide the legal underpinnings upon which rests the current doctrine which excludes most union activities from the jurisdiction of anti-trust laws. This was accomplished in two cases in the early 1940s, *Apex Hosiery* v. *Leader*[2] and *United States* v. *Hutcheson*.[3] In *Apex* the union which was trying to organize the company engaged in a sit-down strike in the firm's plant and refused to allow the company to ship finished goods to out-of-state customers. The Supreme Court ruled that this was not a restraint of commerce, though the circumstances were very similar to those of the justly famous *Danbury Hatters*[4] case (1908), where the union had been found guilty of a Sherman Act violation. The Court's rationale was that the aim of the union in not allowing the goods to be shipped was not to affect commercial competition, but only to obtain appropriate working conditions. In *Hutcheson*, the Carpenters Union instituted a nationwide boycott against the products of the Anheuser-Busch Brewing Company because of a dispute over whether their members or those of the Machinists Union should perform certain work. In the eyes of the Court the legality of this move rested upon: (1) a complicated interreading of Section 20 of the Clayton Act, the Supreme Court's decision in *Duplex-Deering* (1922), and the Norris-LaGuardia Act; and (2) the fact that since an injunction could not be issued against the conduct of the union under the Norris-LaGuardia Act, it should not be held to be illegal. Only one small loophole was left and that was elaborated on in *Allen-Bradley Co.* v. *Local 3, International Brotherhood of Electrical*

---

[2] *Apex Hosiery Co.* v. *Leader*, 310 U.S. 469 (1940); 6 LRRM 647.
[3] *United States* v. *Hutcheson*, 312 U.S. 219 (1946); 7 LRRM 267.
[4] *Loewe* v. *Lawlor*, 208 U.S. 274 (1908).

Workers[5] in 1945. Local 3 had agreements with contractors which called for all equipment to be assembled at the job site and allowed only electrical equipment manufactured in New York City to be used. Since by agreement the contractors included in their bids a percentage of material and labor costs as overhead, the arrangement was beneficial to both parties to the detriment of those who paid for the new construction. The Supreme Court decided that because the union had combined with the firms to restrain trade, the union as well as the firms were guilty of a violation. Had the union policed the conduct of the contractors alone, the case would have had a different ending.

A number of writers feel that the anti-trust laws should be reextended to cover union activity. In some ways they have been, for certain actions like secondary boycotts which were once handled under that section of law are now dealt with by the Taft-Hartley law. In part it is a question of how serious the union's role has been in obtaining monopoly wages. The subject is an important one and probably deserves fuller treatment, though too often it is handled in an overly emotional way. Unfortunately, except when alternative solutions are considered later, we must overlook this question, for its answer would involve several chapters of economic analysis.

THE WAGNER ACT

The Norris-LaGuardia Act is often said to have introduced laissez-faire into federal labor policy. Unions were allowed to utilize any nonviolent economic tactics in their efforts to organize workers; firms were also free to use a host of weapons to resist. Hopefully the best man would win. Three years after this Act was passed, and having little knowledge of the advantages of such a policy, the federal attitude changed from neutrality to more active union participation. Coming at the apex of the New Deal, it was

[5] *Allen-Bradley Co.* v. *Local No. 3, I.B.E.W.*, 325 U.S. 797 (1945); 16 LRRM 798.

perhaps the most radical policy, measured in terms of the extent of the change from the previous position, of any legislation enacted in that turbulent era. Basically it was and still is, a very simple law. It stated that employees had the right of self-organization and, if organized, to bargain collectively with their employers. In order to insure these rights, the law made it an unfair labor practice for an employer to restrain or coerce employees in the exercise of these rights. Further, it required the employer to bargain in good faith with the elected representatives who were to bargain for all the employees in an appropriate bargaining unit regardless of whether or not they belonged to the union. To oversee the operation of the Act, Congress established a National Labor Relations Board composed of three members who were: (1) to pass on the suitability of contested units, and conduct elections to ascertain whether the workers desired to belong to a union and if so to which one; (2) to investigate, prosecute, and judge employer unfair labor practices; and (3) to issue cease and desist orders against conduct found objectionable. The orders were not self-enforcing. For enforcement the Board had to look to the Circuit Courts of Appeals as did those individuals or firms who had been found guilty by the Board and who wished to appeal the decision.

THE TAFT–HARTLEY ACT

Dissatisfaction with a number of aspects of the Wagner Act coupled with the round of wage increases and strikes following World War II led to the passage of the Taft-Hartley Act in 1947. Administratively, it broadened the NLRB from three to five members and placed responsibility for the inauguration of prosecution for unfair labor practices in the hands of a General Counsel who was to be separate from and not answerable to the Board. This change was made to eliminate what some had regarded as the unfairness inherent in the Board acting as prosecutor, judge, and jury. In terms of rights and obligations, the Act retained those rights granted to employees in the Wagner Act, and the obligations of the employer to refrain from coercion and to bargain collectively. In addition, it required unions to refrain from coercion and to bargain in good faith. When the Wagner Act was passed, the difficulty an individual might experience in his efforts to obtain employment because he could not become a member of a particular labor organization or could only become a member upon onerous terms was not apparent. By 1947 the closed shop was recognized as having no real place in a democratic society and was made illegal. In addition, certain restrictions were placed upon the size of initiation fees, and job tenure was protected from lack of union membership except when the employee failed to pay his union dues. Further, states were given the right to prohibit the union shop if they so desired. Thus far, with the exception of the states' right provision on union membership clauses, the only change from the Wagner Act was to place obligations upon unions similar to those placed upon employers. But Congress did not stop there; it added a section devoted to the methods by which a President could deal with labor disputes which threatened the national health and safety. It also moved to make certain classes of union demands illegal. These were union demands: (1) to force an employer or a self-employed person to join a union or an employer organization; (2) to force the employer or any other person to cease dealing in the products of another employer or to cease doing business with any other person; (3) to force an employer to recognize a union if another union had already been made the certified bargaining agent for that unit; and (4) to force an employer to assign particular work to the employees in one union or craft as opposed to another union or craft.

THE LANDRUM–GRIFFIN ACT

This Act is divided into seven parts or titles. Title One is a Bill of Rights for union members. It guarantees every union member equal rights to nominate candidates and to vote in union elections. It also contains certain provisions relative to free speech and assembly with regard to union meetings and regulates the procedure whereby dues may be established. Titles Two through Six concern reports detailing union finances and payments received by union officers, the conduct of trusteeships of subsidiary labor organizations, terms of officers and election procedures, the fiduciary responsibility of union officials, and other minor regulations. Title Seven contains a number of amendments to the Taft-Hartley Act. These serve mainly to clarify the question of federal-state jurisdiction, the voting rights of strikers, and to place tighter restrictions upon union use of secondary boycotts and stranger picketing.

LABOR BOARD JURISDICTION

Under both the Wagner and Taft-Hartley Acts the NLRB was granted jurisdiction over any business which affected interstate commerce. This is the broadest grant which is possible under the commerce clause of the Constitution. The Board has never had the manpower or the budget to fully exercise this broad jurisdiction. Consequently, in 1950, 1954, and again in 1958, it laid down general standards which were intended to exclude purely local business from its supervision. These standards are based upon the type of employer and his volume of business. For retail establishments the gross volume must be $500,000 and for nonretail firms $50,000. The gross volume may be made up of direct inflow or outflow which is defined as goods which flow across state lines between the firm in question and others. Or it may be made up of indirect flows in which the movement is between the firm in question and another firm or firms which are subject to the jurisdiction of the Board. Thus, in *Reliance Fuel*,[6] a local fuel oil distributor came under the Board's supervision on the basis of oil worth $650,000 which was purchased from a major oil company.

Since the Board does not fully exploit its jurisdiction, it is possible for an employer to affect interstate commerce but fail to

[6] *NLRB v. Reliance Fuel Co.*, 371 U.S. 224 (1963); 52 LRRM 2046.

meet the self-imposed standards of the Board. It might be thought that firms like these would be able to avail themselves of the services of state boards. A few years ago this was not true, for the Supreme Court had decided that federal pre-emption of labor-management law as demonstrated by the various laws was such that states were precluded from acting even if the Board refused to do so. This "no man's land" problem as it came to be called was solved by an amendment to the Taft-Hartley Act in 1959. The amendment allows state boards to control areas where the NLRB has not accepted jurisdiction and it further provides that the NLRB must continue to accept its own jurisdictional standards of August 1, 1959. This solution may be less than satisfactory for the firms and unions involved, since only about 30 percent of the states have comprehensive labor codes.

THE OPERATION OF THE NATIONAL
LABOR RELATIONS BOARD

The NLRB is divided into two principal parts, the Board itself and the Office of the General Counsel. The Board maintains 30 regional offices, each with a regional director, regional attorney, staffs of attorneys, and field examiners. When an initial unfair labor practice is filed with a regional office, it is assigned for investigation to a field examiner. If the charge appears to lack merit, it is dismissed or the party bringing the case is asked to withdraw his charge. In cases closed in fiscal 1963, 38.7 percent of the charges were withdrawn and 29.8 percent were dismissed. If the charge is dismissed by the regional office, the plaintiff may ask the General Counsel to review the decision. This is not apt to be fruitful, for less than 10 percent of these appeals to Washington result in the decision being reversed. This low rate reflects the use of an elaborate and formal advice system whereby the more difficult and novel cases are referred to the General Counsel's office in Washington. This insures a degree of uniformity between regions.

If the charge appears to have merit, as is currently true of about 30 percent of the cases received in the regional offices, these offices attempt to have the problem settled informally. In this they are guided by the remedies favored by the Board. About 15 percent of all cases are settled in this manner. After 30 to 45 days, if the charges have not been settled, a formal complaint is issued and the charges are taken to trial before 1 of approximately 60 trial examiners assigned from Washington or San Francisco. Following the completion of his hearing, the trial examiner writes his intermediate report which consists of findings of fact, statements of law, and a proposed remedy. The charged party and the General Counsel can either accept this or file exceptions with the Board. Exceptions are filed in about 85 percent of the cases. When exceptions are filed, the NLRB is required to decide the case.

The Board will normally issue its own decision on the basis of the written record, although in a few very important or novel cases it may allow the parties time for oral argument. The decision of the NLRB may be made by the full five-man Board or by a panel of three members. In fiscal 1963 the Board issued 1306 decisions. Of these 905 were unfair labor practice cases, 227 were decisions involving questions of representation, and 40 determinations of job assignments in jurisdictional disputes were made. The decisions of this Board are not self-enforcing. If a party refuses to abide by the remedy, the NLRB must seek a court order from a U.S. Circuit Court of Appeals. In like manner, a party who feels that the decision was incorrect may appeal his case to that same court.

In 1963 the Appeals Court decided 198 NLRB cases. In 113 cases the orders were enforced in full, while 34 more were partially enforced. Seven cases were partially remanded, sent back to the NLRB for the determination of additional facts, and partially enforced, while 7 more were remanded in their entirety. Finally, in 34 cases, the orders of the Board were set aside.

In addition to unfair labor practices, the Board conducts elections to determine whether employees wish to be represented. Until a few years ago all election decisions were made by the

Board in Washington. Now the bulk of the work is done by the regional directors, with Washington handling only appeals from their decisions. In fiscal 1963 there were 10,333 petitions for elections and 648 petitions for decertification elections. Nine percent of these were dismissed and 25 percent were withdrawn leaving a total of 7240 cases, requiring that an election be ordered. Of these only 153 or 1.5 percent were ordered by the full Board in Washington. Of the 6871 collective bargaining elections actually held, 5150 or almost three-quarters were conducted under voluntary agreements of the parties. Ninety percent of those eligible to vote did so. Sixty percent of the votes cast were for representation and this resulted in unions winning 59 percent or 4052 elections. In the 225 decertification elections to determine if the employees still wished to be represented by a union, unions won only 26.6 percent. The results in these new elections might be compared to those 10 and 20 years ago. In 1953 unions won 71.9 percent of the elections and in 1943 they won 86.9 percent.

With this brief review of the principal legislation and the operations of the NLRB as a background, it is possible to proceed to a discussion of some of the substantive issues. Before turning to these, however, it seems wise to devote some time to a consideration of other aspects of the framework within which substantive decisions are made. These aspects are:

1. The many facets of public policy.
2. The meaning of the public interest which policies seek to fulfill.
3. Some characteristics of our legal system.
4. The historical evolution of labor legislation.
5. Some of the things which must be considered when the decision process of public authorities is studied.

These are considered in the next four chapters.

Suggested Readings

Annual Report of the National Labor Relations Board, Washington: U.S. Government Printing Office.
Wesley M. Wilson, *Labor Law Handbook*, New York: Bobbs-Merrill, 1963.

CHAPTER 2

Public Policy
and Public Interest

_____

WHAT IS PUBLIC POLICY?

Before a meaningful examination of the rationale and appropriateness of specific applications of policy can be accomplished, it is desirable to clarify the words "public policy" and "public interest." The many dimensions of policy are discussed in the first section of this chapter and a definition of the "public interest" is contained in the second section.

A traditional beginning for a discussion of policy based upon legislation is with the wording of the statute. Indeed, it is sometimes thought that the words of the law reflect the reality of policy, just as many believe the federal income tax to be highly progressive simply because the marginal tax rate rises to 70 percent. Yet, in 1958 when the marginal rate rose to a high of 93 percent, only 12 percent of the revenue collected came from taxpayers whose average rate exceeded 20 percent. So too with policy; the statute can only be the beginning. As an illustration, consider the duty to bargain which is set out in Section 8 d of the Taft-Hartley Act.

For the purposes of this section, to bargain collectively is the performance of the mutual obligation of the employer and the representative of the employees to meet at reasonable times and confer in
good faith with respect to the wages, hours, and other terms and conditions of employment, or the negotiation of an agreement, or any
question arising thereunder, and the execution of a written contract
incorporating any agreement reached if requested by either party, but
such obligation does not compel either party to agree to a proposal
or require the making of a concession: . . .

These words seem alive with indecision. How many times must
one meet in order to have met at reasonable times? What is a
condition of employment? Does it include a Christmas bonus, the
firm's location of new plants, etc.? From these questions it is an
easy step to go beyond the mere statute to a recognition of the role
of the NLRB in framing and guiding the law. At a minimum, such
an authority should clarify the meaning contained in the congressional intent—or as its life-long critics of various political hues
have argued, it will completely subvert the *clear intent* of the
Congress. Decisions by the Board are reviewable in the federal
courts of appeals, adding a third force to the policy workshop.
In fact, the NLRB has more business in these courts than all other
federal administrative agencies combined.

Were these the only factors involved, the cases could be com-
partmentalized by subject matter, date of occurrence, size of firm,
etc. Then, from these variables, a probability statement of federal
policy could be developed. One would obtain the following: Were
the ABC manufacturing company to engage in the following acts
. . . , the probability is .X that ABC would be held to have committed an unfair labor practice. The results of such an approach,
despite Justice Frankfurter's remarks in *Carpenters Union* v.
NLRB[1] ". . . Construing legislation . . . could not be accomplished by the subtlest of modern 'brain' machines" would be ones
which would inspire reasonable confidence. There would always be

[1] *Local 1976, Carpenters Union* v. NLRB, 357 U.S. 93 at 100 (1957); 42
LRRM 2243 at 2246.

some cases which wouldn't fit, as perhaps illustrated by the following example. A client asked his lawyer for a list of all the "anti-union" activities which did not violate the law in which he could engage during a union organizing drive. The attorney made the list, the employer acted upon it, the union filed charges, and the Board decided in the union's favor. The lawyer was enraged and complained to the Board. He received a reply to the effect that, it is true that you followed all of the cases, all, that is, but one, the one we decided just before yours.

The Courts and the Board are not the only participants; a number of others must also be considered. One of these is the regional office of the NLRB. When an unfair labor practice charge is filed with a regional office of the NLRB, it is investigated by that office to see whether the charge merits a formal complaint. On the basis of this investigation, the regional office requests the party to withdraw the charge, suggests and approves the disposition of an informal settlement, or seeks the issuance of a formal complaint. In so doing, the regional office has made decisions in the three principal areas requiring decisions under the Act: legality of the respondent's action, sufficiency of facts, and type of remedy.

Consider a routine case: A union organizer is fired by a company. At the time of the discharge the company was unaware of the individual's union activity; nothing else in the company's conduct is indicative of an anti-union bias. In such a situation no complaint over the discharge would be upheld by the NLRB or the courts. Policy is, therefore, not affected by having the decision made in a regional office rather than being made by the Board after a formal proceeding. The undetermined but real role of the regional staff comes in those cases where the factual situations are hazy and in areas which are new or changing and in which, consequently, the views of the members of the NLRB are not yet firm and clear. In these instances, there is ample opportunity for the regional offices to play active roles in the determination of policy, especially as it affects a particular firm, individual, or union.

When the prosecution of unfair labor practices was separated from the other duties of the NLRB by the establishment of the Office of the General Counsel in the Taft-Hartley amendments to the Wagner Act, Congress added still another actor to policy determination. The General Counsel plays a primary role in determining new directions in labor policy since his office determines whether to prosecute in situations involving actions whose legality has not been tested by prior Board decisions. His crucial role is strengthened by the fact that his refusal to issue a complaint is not considered a final order of the NLRB and consequently his decision is not reviewable by an appeals court. In addition to this type of control, there are other factors, some of which are illustrated in the following statement by a former General Counsel, Stuart Rothman.

I was urged to issue a complaint on the theory that a union's strike for an exclusive hiring hall clause in a contract was illegal because such a clause was not a mandatory subject for bargaining. While prior Board precedent supported the view that such a clause was a mandatory subject, the Board's *Mountain Pacific* decision gave some support to a contrary view. It was argued by some, without regard to an overall consideration of the consequences, that complaint should have issued merely because the question was in doubt. . . . The fact that long established relationships would be shaken and that prolonged litigation involving great expenditure of time, money and energy would ensue was disregarded or considered of small moment.

I felt, on the other hand, that proceeding to complaint was unwarranted in view of the problem overall.

The unsettling consequences in large and important segments of our industry . . . the doubt that a violation of law existed under prior precedents and the fact that the *Mountain Pacific* doctrine itself was before the Supreme Court, were some factors considered. I felt that the decision to be made did not involve a merely technical question of law but rather raised far-reaching consequences requiring insights into the problem overall.[2]

[2] *Administration of the Labor-Management Relations Act by the NLRB,* Hearings before the Subcommittee on National Labor Relations Board of the Committee on Education and Labor, House of Representatives, 87th Cong., 1st Sess., 1961, pp. 1154–1155. (Hereafter cited as Pucinski.)

If the rule to issue complaints in all cases where there is any question of a possible violation is rejected, as it was by Mr. Rothman, what rule should the General Counsel follow? Stated alternatively, how many cases should the Office of the General Counsel win? Should it take only those where, clearly, a violation has occurred and thereby win the vast majority of the cases which it prosecutes? Or should it take every case where there is a reasonable chance that the Board will agree that there is a violation?

In 1961 Mr. Rothman, in testimony before the House Subcommittee investigating the NLRB, stated that his Office's view was being upheld in about 77 out of every 100 cases it initiated. And since, during his term, a greater number of complaints per initial charge were being issued than had been issued previously, it is probable that an even "better" won-and-lost record was maintained by earlier General Counsels.[3] There is, of course, no easy way to determine what the appropriate level of withdrawals and dismissals and the related winning percentage in hearings before trial examiners and the Board should be. There will always be instances where the witnesses cannot be found, where they have lied to the union representative who filed the charge, and so forth. There will also be instances where parties will bring charges that they know will not result in a formal complaint being issued. In such instances the charge is filed to delay an election, to impress the faithful, or to bring indirect legal pressure upon the employer or the union. There will also be situations in which it seems clear that the employer has discharged an employee in violation of the Act, but in which the employer has an excellent defense because the employee has, by his job-related activities, given the employer ample grounds for the discharge. Still, since more violators of the Act will be caught if the General Counsel wins 35 percent of his cases than if he wins 85 percent, it is clear that the impact of policy will vary to the extent that the General Counsel does or does not take the marginal case.

Up to now we have treated the charging and charged parties as

[3] The General Counsel's batting average is found in Pucinski, p. 1087.

completely passive, except insofar as they choose to initiate charges
with the NLRB or to maintain records which might be useful in
working out a case. There are other ways in which the parties can
affect the impact of federal policy. Charges not really intended to
be complaints and filing of unfair labor practice charges to prevent or delay the holding of a representation election have already
been mentioned. There is also the question of whether a charge
is to be informally settled or carried through all possible steps of
litigation. There is, to my knowledge, no information on whether
a form of bargaining takes place between employers and unions
relative to informal compliance. Its existence would not be surprising considering the vast time difference between the two types
of solutions. An informal settlement may be obtained in the 30
to 45 days between the determination that the charges have merit
and the issuance of a formal complaint. A case going before the
Board will take almost a year or even longer. On April 28, 1961,
the oldest quartile of cases then before the NLRB had been filed
between November 15, 1957 and June 6, 1960. About 30 percent
of all formal NLRB orders are appealed beyond the Board to the
federal courts and this adds another year or so. An example of
possible bargaining appears in the *Sun Ray Drug*[4] case. The employer had discharged several employees for what he termed
legitimate reasons. A preliminary investigation indicated that the
case had merit and a complaint was issued on January 12, 1959.
A formal hearing opened on February 17, 1959. The following
day an informal settlement calling for the posting of notices, offer
of reinstatement, and full back pay was executed at the insistence
of the union even though the counsel for the NLRB urged a formal
settlement stipulation or completion of the hearing.

The possibilities for delay available to a company which does
not wish to bargain with a union are almost endless and involve a
number of technical points. The following example indicates some
of them. The employer, to the extent possible, forces a Board
determination of the appropriate unit by insisting that certain

[4] *Sun Ray Drug*, 5 CA 1438; Pucinski, 1265.

employees be included or excluded. However, since most of the questions regarding elections have been delegated to the Regional Directors, this procedure is no longer as fruitful for delay as it once was. During the pre-election period the employer's conduct strays over the permissible so that the election is nullified if the union loses. Before a new election is held, the employer fires a leading union organizer. This unfair labor practice charge must be settled before a second election may be held. By limiting himself to one employee, the back pay cost of the eventual Court of Appeals order to reinstate is minimized. An election is held, the union wins, but the company refuses to bargain on the grounds of an improper unit decision. At last the Court of Appeals, after another Board determination, forces the employer to bargain. This time there is bargaining, but only a few hours a week, and the answer is always no. Another unfair labor practice charge then moves through the administrative machinery. Assuming a decision against the employer, his strategy will be to ignore it and wait until he is at last faced with a contempt citation. Then, and only then, will he begin to bargain in earnest. By now the union has probably disappeared and five to ten years may have elapsed. It is true that the Act does give the Board some power in a case like this since it could seek a court order to force the employer to behave during the time the subsequent unfair labor practices are being heard. But the Board's use of its discretionary injunctive power to prevent continued employer or union refusal to behave has been limited.

At the beginning of this section, we noted that it is necessary to look beyond the mere statements in the United States Code if federal labor policy is to be known. As has been seen, a number of formal organizations and individuals, including the parties themselves, play a strong role in shaping the intent of those who drafted and voted for the code provisions. It would be naïve to assume that merely because, under a given set of circumstances, the ABC manufacturing company's actions result in a particular court order means that the desired policy of the Act has in some way been sustained. Does the fact that a given percentage of all discharged employees are re-employed with back wages really make them willing to exercise their rights as outlined in the Act? The answer to this requires going into the field and finding what happens after the final order is handed down. Too little of this sort of inquiry has been undertaken and some of the little that has been done does not answer the central question of what the economic impact of the orders has been. Thus, it may be, as the Board has noted, that 75 to 90 percent (depending upon the stage) of all duty to bargain cases in fiscal 1961 resulted in signed contracts, but the interesting question is what are the extra rights or privileges enjoyed by employees who won?

WHAT IS THE PUBLIC INTEREST?

In later chapters the discussions will center on specific policies and their implications. One of the questions to be raised is whether certain policies are good or desirable. Before answering, other than in terms of one's own feelings, it would be desirable if some framework could be provided by which the extent to which these policies are in the public interest could be judged. It is to this that we now turn.

How is the public interest defined? Who is this public? Or in the words of the poet Carl Sandburg:

> Who shall speak for the People?
> Who has the answers?
> Where is the sure interpreter?
> Who knows what to say?[5]

An answer as to what the public interest is may be sought at various levels of generality. Most proposed solutions are of the broadest possible nature and provide few guides with which to

[5] Carl Sandburg, *The People, Yes,* New York: Harcourt Brace & World, 1936, p. 38.

judge specific labor policies. As an example, the authors of *The Public Interest in National Labor Policy* stress that,

A fundamental goal by which to judge all processes is that of freedom of individual choice, . . . We seek a society in which individuals may decide for themselves how best to use their abilities and in which individuals receive respect, dignity, and recognition for their achievements.[6]

Perhaps all of us could subscribe to the statement above, yet how does it indicate the limits of each individual's choice when they are not mutually independent?

The railroad dispute over work rules which was settled in 1964 is a good example of the perplexing problem of prescribing a public interest for specific situations. In the summer of 1963, the President told the parties that, "If no settlement is reached in this case, there will be no alternative to the enactment of new legislation which will protect the public. . . ." The import of his words is clear; the public interest places less value upon the freedom of the parties to the railroad dispute to determine their own conditions of employment than it does upon the public right to the uninterrupted services of the railroads. What is not clear is the basis for this decision. Would the same thing be true for all industries or only for the railroads? How does one draw the line between industries which would be included and those which would be excluded? Also, the President's formulation of the public interest does not prescribe between alternative methods which legislation might prescribe for solving the railroad dispute.

Advice and counsel on how to formulate the public interest is not lacking. On one side might be found Edmund Burke and those who argue with him that there exists a specific and knowable national or public interest and, further, that it can be determined.

. . . It is not a *congress* of ambassadors from different and hostile interests, which interests each must maintain, as an agent and advo-

[6] An Independent Study Group, *The Public Interest in National Labor Policy*, Committee for Economic Development, 1960, pp. 51–52.

cate, against other agents and advocates; but Parliament is a *deliberative* assembly of *one* nation, with *one* interest, that of the whole—where not local purposes, not local prejudices ought to guide, but the general good, resulting from the general reason of the whole. You choose a member, indeed; but when you have chosen him, he is not a member from Bristol, but is a member of *Parliament*.[7]

On another side are those like the authors of the *Federalist Papers*, who, with Burke, see clearly articulated and known interests, but only those of subsets within the society.

A landed interest, a manufacturing interest, a mercantile interest, a moneyed interest, with many lesser interests, grow up of necessity in civilized nations, and divide them into different classes, actuated by different sentiments and views. The regulation of these various and interfering interests forms the principal task of modern legislation, and involves the spirit of party and faction in the necessary and ordinary operations of government.[8]

Though many probably share Burke's belief in the singleness of the public interest, a recognition of diverse interests is probably more consistent with a concern over general policies for particular types of problems. Thus, we are seemingly forced in the direction of Hamilton, Jay, and Madison. But, are we better served? We are aware of conflicting interests, and we know that within the political process these interests will in some manner or means accommodate themselves to one another. But, are the answers thus generated in the public interest? Were we strict majoritarians, our reply would be yes. Yet, though we submit in many respects to majority rule situations, it is probably true that all of us recognize overriding minority interests and are not willing to completely reverse a gem of conventional wisdom and accept as correct "Might makes Right." Our problem, if not the solution, is now clear.

[7] Edmund Burke, *The Writings and Speeches of Edmund Burke*, Boston: Little, Brown, 1901, Vol. II, p. 96.
[8] *The Federalist on the New Constitution*, Hallowell: Masters, Smith and Co., 1852, Vol. I, No. 10, p. 44.

What is needed is some rule which accords due deference to those solutions and situations which should be guided by the majority of the moment and those which must give way to minority considerations.

Instead of trying to define the public interest in terms of over-all or group terms, perhaps it will be easier to determine our rule if the emphasis is upon the individual. If individuals can be assumed to have a policy position on all questions, then what is needed is some formulation which will express the "best" policy in terms of the individual beliefs. The development of such a criterion is essentially what economists have attempted with their social welfare functions. This means that unless our formulation is merely to utilize some form of majority or weighted majority rule, our results will be very similar to those of the economist. We must be willing to compare the policy positions of various individuals and decide which position should have greater value. For example, a Negro's right to be served is more important than that of an owner of public accommodations to select his customers by any arbitrary system. In other words, we shall have to define the public interest as those policies in which the gains for some are obtained without losses to others, or where those who gain compensate those who lose. Referring to the above example, this would mean that all who believe in equal rights would now have to pay segregationists because they are no longer allowed to discriminate.

There are three objections which can be raised to a formulation which states that a policy is in the public interest if the gains which it generates for some individuals are obtained without losses to others, or one in which the losers receive compensation from the gainers. Perhaps the most important objection is that it assumes away the problem of the initial distribution. If, as some of its supporters claimed, the Taft-Hartley law marked a return to a federal labor law which was balanced between the interests of labor and of management, the above formulation might be an appropriate one with which to judge proposed amendments. Certainly supporters of the Taft-Hartley law would not have accepted such a formulation in 1946 nor would their opposition have accepted it in 1934. A second objection is the difficulty associated with the payment and receipt of compensation with our current political and ethical beliefs. An example is the inability of labor to secure legislation to overturn the Supreme Court's decision in the *Denver Building Trades Case*[9] (1951). In that case the Supreme Court decided that even though employees of different contractors engaged in construction at a common site worked together in much the same way that employees in different departments of a commonly operated factory work, a picket line directed against one employer was not grounds for employees of the other contractors to refuse to work. The decision had its principal impact upon firms and unions in the construction industry and the unions tried for many years to obtain an amendment to the law so that a common situs of work would be treated as if it were operated by a single employer. In the middle of the Eisenhower administration, the building trades and the construction industry at last agreed upon a common bill. Even the administration approved it, but by then some industrial unions had also become concerned over certain aspects of the proposed legislation and they and the craft unions were unable to agree on a single bill. Congress then refused to act, for its members were not desirous of gaining enemies in the ranks of labor, regardless of the provisions of the amendment. Had monetary payments in these circumstances been an allowable practice, one group of unions could have paid the other group to give up their opposition to the bill. A final objection, especially for our concern, is the inability to specify what different individuals' policy preferences are so that conclusions concerning specific policies can be achieved.

While not providing a solution, the individualistic approach does suggest some lines of thought whose exploration may be fruitful. One of these is why complete unanimity is not a better political

---

[9] *NLRB* v. *Denver Building and Construction Trades Council,* 341 U.S. 675 (1951); 28 LRRM 2108.

solution than majority rule. Here, the compensation rule would have to be allowed to work, for side payments would be necessary to obtain the support of those whose interests would not be favored by whatever was being proposed. One difficulty with this would be the cost of obtaining agreement. This suggests that an individual would favor a system in which the net costs, if any, he expected to incur from being on the losing side of policy decisions would be counterbalanced by the gains associated with a lower cost of reaching agreement. Since, in many ways, majority rule fits this equilibrium for homogeneous populations, it is not surprising that it is so widely used. It also indicates why those who expect to be associated more often with the minority rather than the majority prefer a greater degree of unanimity. Conversely, it suggests why members of the Communist party approve of its minority rule. Nor is such a system at great variance with the way policy is determined in this country. Broad areas of policy are settled, at least nominally, by simple majority rule, but always subject to the protection of due process and minority constitutional rights by a judicial tribunal. In addition, there are important areas where majority agreement is not followed as in amending of federal and state constitutions, zoning law changes, etc. Thus it is perhaps not an incorrect conclusion that some special concern is felt with regard to changing the rules of the game as opposed to the specific elaboration of the value of those rules at various times. If this is true, does it allow us to define the public interest, not in terms of what specific policies should be but in terms of the methods by which the specific policies should be decided? If we define the public interest in these terms, does this provide a public interest which will allow us to judge specific policies? In the sense in which Justice Roberts spoke of the duty of the court, "To lay the article of the Constitution which is invoked beside the statute which is challenged and to decide whether the latter squares with the former,"[10] our answer must be no. Yet, within the context of our country's history, we may be able to say that

[10] *United States* v. *Butler*, 297 U.S. 1 (1936) at 62–63.

the public interest is that which commands majority support at the time, subject to the constraint of reasonable minority rights and includes a disinclination to change the basic rules of the game. This elaboration of what constitutes the public interest suggests that the specific policies of any time will not represent a consensus—for that does not exist—but rather will represent the desire of a shifting majority. We may, however, find more consensus when it comes to changing the rules of the game.

Suggested Readings

Edward C. Banfield, *Political Influence*, Glencoe, Ill.: The Free Press, 1961.

James M. Buchanan and Gordon Tullock, *The Calculus of Consent*, Ann Arbor: University of Michigan Press, 1962. &

Jerome Rothenberg, *The Measurement of Social Welfare*, Englewood Cliffs, N.J.: Prentice-Hall, 1961.

Paul A. Samuelson, "Modern Economic Realities and Individualism," *The Texas Quarterly*, Summer, 1963, pp. 128–139.

Glendon Schubert, *The Public Interest*, Glencoe, Ill.: The Free Press, 1960.

CHAPTER 3

The Law

Common law, statute law, and administrative regulations within the framework of the Constitution form the structure of our legal system within which much of federal labor policy is developed. Consequently, an understanding of policy is enhanced by some knowledge of that system. Only the briefest beginning can be accomplished in a single chapter, but at least some of the ideas and concepts which are necessary to such an understanding may be suggested.

COMMON LAW

The strands of history which have been woven into our legal system are drawn from many sources. Chief and dominant among them is English common law. The ultimate origins of this law may have been rooted in pre-Norman history. The champions of common law in the sixteenth and seventeenth centuries saw it as derived from the freemen of pre-Saxon England. But basically it derives from feudal custom associated with the Anglo-Norman king's tenants-in-chief. It was based upon the fundamental notion of fealty as associated with land tenure. The essence of what was to become common law was the absolute right of the freeman to his property, whatever the demands or needs of the king.

This dominant position of land law was fortified during the Middle Ages by a generally accepted belief that the positive law of any society acquired sanction from divine law. Laws were not passed, they existed, and over a long period of time they became recognized. This meant that legislatures, as we know them, were unnecessary, and the older the precedents behind a decision, the more honorable the holding. In this tradition, the education of those who came to have a primary role in shaping the law served to strengthen the emphasis upon maintaining the logic of prior decisions. Basic to medieval learning was dialectic, based upon Aristotelian logic as opposed to historical or comparative scholarship. The primary role of deductive knowledge required an authority for the major premise; hence, in later years, the initial reverence for Aristotle, Peter Lombard, and Hippocrates was extended to numerous lesser figures. An example of the extent to which this divorced knowledge from reality is that, in the medical education of Paris, doctors preferred to dispute about diseases in impeccable syllogisms rather than to examine live patients with real diseases.

From this emphasis upon form developed a law which placed extreme reliance upon form as opposed to substance. When a contract was drawn up, signed, and sealed, it existed only as long as the sealed copy existed. And it existed even if a man's seal had been put to the paper without his knowledge. Richard III once asked whether there would be a recourse for the individual or the king if someone brought a false writ and action against a man who was thereby imprisoned and died. The answer was no, for the trial had not been completed. In the same way, a misspelled word could void an entire trial, a policy not unknown in this country. It was once held (Texas) that a verdict of guilty in the "fist" degree was of no effect. Another Texas case is also interesting. Bob White was an illiterate Negro who was accused of raping a white woman. One night he was taken into the woods by the Texas Rangers, whipped, and ultimately, by third-degree methods, forced to confess. During his trial the prosecutor said, "Look at this court room: it is crowded with Polk county people demanding the death penalty for Bob White." For this remark, but never for the way in which the confession was obtained, the Texas Court of Criminal Appeals reversed the first conviction.[1]

As a reaction to the emphasis upon form, the degree of corruption which seemed to grow up around the common law courts, and most powerfully, to the basic inability of a law built upon relationships associated with land tenure to deal with the rising needs of a commercial class, there arose repeated attempts to utilize the king's courts, whose standards were justice or equity. The success of the king's courts in providing equity and the struggle between them and the common law courts varied through the years. We may conclude that: (1) even today a dispute still exists as to whether a court's primary function is to see that the form of the law is maintained or to see that justice is done; and (2) that the concept of equity which was originally set up to protect common people from an outdated legal system became, in the late nineteenth century, a vehicle which greatly hindered the development of unions.

THE CONSTITUTION AND THE SUPREME COURT

Common laws, statutes, and administrative regulations all exist within the broader context of our Constitution. The resulting system is held together, in part, by the fact that ultimately all are subject to interpretation by a single unit, the Supreme Court. Because of its unique position, some consideration should be given to the Court's nature and history.

The role and position of the Supreme Court do not follow simply from the concepts of the founding fathers. Rather, the role and position represent a complex historical evolution. Most

[1] *Bob White* v. *Texas*, 308 U.S. 631 (1940).

amendments to the Constitution are either basic protections of enduring rights or a manifestation of profound social movements, e.g., prohibition. In these contexts, the Eleventh Amendment which states:

> The judicial power of the United States shall not be construed to extend to any suit in law or equity, commenced or prosecuted against one of the United States by citizens of another State, or by citizens or subjects of any foreign state

seems strangely out of place. It is, however, a monument to a long-standing division in our country's attitude toward a Supreme Court and the role it should play in our society, and to the complex mixture of standard appellate jurisdiction and political policy-making which has characterized the Court's history. An innocent visitor from another planet, learning of the recent decisions on racial discrimination and apportionment would be quite mistaken if he concluded that the basis for the power wielded by these nine men was deeply rooted in American political dogma. The Constitution merely mentions the Supreme Court, saying that there shall be one and that its power will extend to all cases in law and equity arising under the Constitution, and that its appellate jurisdiction is subject to such regulations as Congress may decide to make. The Judiciary Act of 1789, although a little clearer, still contains no explicit statement concerning the relative role of the Congress and the Court in disagreements over the constitutionality of a statute. The statements of the Constitutional Convention, and the ratification controversy may be searched in vain for a precise indication of where the power to determine constitutionality was to rest. The right, then, of the Supreme Court to declare the acts of state and federal governments unconstitutional was not clearly granted, but has been slowly built up over a long period of years.

Several factors seem to have played an important role in the process by which the Court acquired its power. First, as the power of early common law was enhanced by the beliefs of many people concerning the role of God in setting out the *law*, so too the rationale for revolution stemming from the will or consent of the governed was strengthened by the concept of a constitutionalism which had been overstepped by the king, thus justifying revolution against his authority.

. . . The Supreme Legislature derives its power and authority from the constitution, it cannot overleap the bounds of it, without destroying its own foundation; that the Constitution ascertains and limits both sovereignty and allegiance.[2]

The public, used to thinking in terms of both popular will and fundamental limitations, was ripe for the development which followed.

A second factor was the evolutionary manner in which the Court's influence was allowed to unfold. Judge Wilson's decision, in *Chisholm* v. *Georgia*[3] in 1793, that, as to the purpose of union, Georgia was not a sovereign state and could be sued for recovery of debt by citizens of another state, was too strong. The Eleventh Amendment resulted from this decision.

After Chief Justice Marshall joined the Court in 1801, bold federal decisions became more muted. This muted quality is beautifully illustrated in *Marbury* v. *Madison*,[4] generally considered the cornerstone for the Supreme Court's authority over the Constitution. Marbury received from President Adams a midnight appointment as a Justice of the Peace. His commission was signed, sealed, but undelivered when Adams's term ended, but Jefferson would not allow the commission to be delivered. Marbury requested a court order (writ of mandamus) to force Madison, Jefferson's Secretary of State, to deliver the document. When the case reached the Supreme Court, Marshall's decision upheld Mar-

[2] The statement is by Samuel Adams as quoted in Loren P. Beth, *Politics, the Constitution and the Supreme Court*, New York: Harper & Row, 1963, p. 7.

[3] *Chisholm* v. *Georgia*, 2 Dallas 419 (1793).

[4] *Marbury* v. *Madison*, 1 Cranch 137 (1803).

bury's right to the commission, but held that the Court could not grant the writ because the law (Judiciary Act of 1789) giving the Supreme Court original jurisdiction in matters like this violated the Constitution. Marshall said:

If, then, the courts are to regard the Constitution, and the Constitution is superior to any ordinary act of the legislature, the Constitution, and not such ordinary act, must govern the case to which both apply. Those then who controvert the principle that the Constitution is to be considered, in court, as a paramount law, are reduced to the necessity of maintaining that courts must close their eyes on the Constitution, and see only the law.

He then went on to illustrate the subject by reference to constitutional provisions against interstate duties, ex post facto laws, and the requirement of two witnesses or confession in open court for conviction of treason. The rhetorical question was asked of what decision should be made by a Court, were Congress to pass a law saying that a single witness in a treason trial was sufficient. The answer is clear and one is thus led to Marshall's conclusion "that a law repugnant to the Constitution is void; and that courts, as well as other departments are bound by that instrument."

The decision is also notable for what it does not say. Those who believed in the superiority of the legislature upon constitutional questions were not concerned with clearly worded clauses like two witnesses, for Congress would never pass such legislation. Their concern was with sections, like the commerce clause, whose extent and coverage were far from clearly delineated. For sections like these, the question of whether the Court or the Congress should decide whether a specific law was consistent with the Constitution's general guide was a meaningful one. This was the first time that an act of any legislature, and the only federal law, until the one involved in the Dred Scott decision many years later, was declared unconstitutional. Note the irony, the keystone in judicial control of constitutionality begins with a voluntary restriction of judicial power.

Seven years after *Marbury* v. *Madison* a state law was declared unconstitutional. The case of *Fletcher* v. *Peck*[5] concerned the "splendid" Yazoo land grand scandal. Briefly, without going into the details, the state of Georgia in 1795 sold for a very low price most of what now constitutes the states of Alabama and Mississippi. All but one of the legislators who voted for the sale had been bribed. A subsequent legislature rescinded the grant, but not until after land had been resold to many innocent third parties. The question at the bar was whether Georgia could now rescind its earlier action. The answer was no.

A third factor in the Court's success was the inability of its opponents to focus upon the appropriate question. The Eleventh Amendment still stands as a monument to those who were opposed to a strong federal judiciary, but typically the main current of opposition was wasted in undue concern over the particular decision rather than with the right of the Court to have made any decision in the case in point. In *McCulloch* v. *Maryland*,[6] which upheld the right of Congress to establish a National Bank and forbade the states from using their powers of taxation to limit the rights of the federal government, the reaction to the decision was favorable in the North which supported the Bank, but less so in the South and the West which were more hostile. Even in Virginia where Spencer Roane of the Virginia Court of Appeals had held that the meaning of the federal Constitution was for state courts to decide, opposition was to the constitutionality of the Bank rather than to the right of the Court to decide that question. The story is repeated again and again. In *Gibbons* v. *Ogden*[7] (1824) which ended a steamboat monopoly, the result was hailed and the broad reach of the commerce clause, which has a distinctly twentieth-century quality, was largely ignored. So too in our own day. Those of the far right who would curb the Court propose a super court of the 50 chief justices of the state supreme

[5] *Fletcher* v. *Peck*, 6 Cranch 87 (1810).
[6] *McCulloch* v. *Maryland*, 4 Wheaton 316 (1819).
[7] *Gibbons* v. *Ogden*, 9 Wheaton 1 (1824).

courts. Their desire is not the elimination of judicial power but a hope for more conservative opinions.

Also important has been a seeming willingness by the Court to avoid extended opposition to positions supported by an over-whelming majority of the public. This willingness may best be illustrated by the Court's wartime behavior. Early in the Civil War President Lincoln suspended the operation of habeas corpus. Subsequent to that order a Maryland secessionist who was being held in a military prison obtained a writ of habeas corpus for his release. The general in command of the prison refused to honor it. The Supreme Court then held the general to be in contempt of court. A marshal was sent to arrest the general, but the marshal was not allowed into the fort and an appeal to President Lincoln to enforce the Court order brought no answer. The Court, how-ever, found reason to refuse jurisdiction in matters like the trial of civilians by military commissions and the legal tender acts. Then, with the war over, nine justices with a flourish in *Ex Parte Milligan*[8] decided that not only had Congress denied the military the right to try civilians, but that Congress did not even have the power to allow military trials of civilians during wartime.

Such "timidity" ("wisdom") found many years ago is still in evidence. One of the blackest acts in United States history con-cerns the removal of 112,000 Japanese, 70,000 of them U.S. citizens against whom no crime could be charged, let alone proved, from areas of the West Coast in the early days of World War II. The details which lie behind the action are sordid at best, illustrating the worst of racial prejudice, greed, and inexcusable neglect of duty; but here we shall limit ourselves to the role of the Court. The initial case was *Hiraboyashi* v. *U.S.*,[9] which tested the right of the military to impose an indiscriminate curfew upon Japanese citizens. This the Court upheld, reasoning that, due to the par-ticular circumstances of the times, such an infraction of civil rights did not seem so great when contrasted to the pressing

---

[8] *Ex Parte Milligan*, 4 Wallace 2 (1866).
[9] *Hiraboyashi* v. *United States*, 320 U.S. 81 (1942).

public necessity, but it noted that such reasoning applied only to the curfew and not beyond. Unfortunately this limitation was lost when review of the exclusion orders came up in *Korematsu* v. *U.S.*:[10]

> We cannot reject as unfounded the judgment of the military authorities that there were disloyal members of the population whose number and strength cannot be precisely and quickly ascertained. We cannot say that the war-making branches of the government did not have ground for believing . . .

Yet no evidence to support such judgments was ever presented, none was ever found afterward, even in Hawaii, where, though the rationale might have been stronger, the population was never moved.

In its role of arbiter of the Constitution, the Court has evolved through three general eras. As might be anticipated, the years before the Civil War are chiefly characterized by state-federal relationships. With these relationships to a major degree settled by that War, the Court's attention turned to questions of economic regulation. In the *Slaughter House Cases*[11] of 1873 the Court held (5–4) that the Fourteenth Amendment did not protect a citizen of a state against the legislative power of his own state. In other words, the protections against federal power contained in the Bill of Rights did not now through the Fourteenth Amendment provide protection against the legislative power of a man's own state. Three years later in *Munn* v. *Illinois*[12] citizens were held to be protected against any encroachment upon "an acknowledged right of citizenship by the legislatures of the States," but the minority position that among these rights was a liberal construction of the words "deprive any person of . . . property without due process of law" was not explicitly recognized. In time this concept was recognized and by 1897 "liberty of contract" was

[10] *Korematsu* v. *United States*, 323 U.S. 214 (1944) at 216.
[11] *Slaughter House Cases*, 16 Wallace 36 (1873).
[12] *Munn* v. *Illinois*, 94 U.S. 113 (1876).

firmly in the Constitution where, in a sense, it was to remain for 40 years. In 1937, following the depression, the 1936 elections, and Roosevelt's court-packing plan, the Court upheld the Wagner Act, and thereby retired from its economic stewardship. Its new concern, plainly evident today, became the rights of minorities. In passing, it should be noted that, though the Court's vigorous support of Herbert Spencer and laissez-faire hampered the growth of unions, its subsequent concern for minority rights might well have been impossible without its earlier defense of the business community, for in this defense the Supreme Court gave a broad interpretation to the Fourteenth Amendment.

LABOR LAW AND THE COURTS

In upholding the constitutionality of the Wagner Act, when many confidently predicted that it would not, the Court began what has been its very important role in the development of federal labor policy. Before considering its specific contributions in later chapters, some attention should be given to the process out of which these contributions evolve.

The Wagner and Taft-Hartley Acts have given the NLRB wide discretion in the determination of the contexts and specific constellations of conduct which constitute inappropriate actions and unfair labor practices. In one sense Congress can be viewed as having said, "Our policy is thus—go and see that justice is done." This attitude would mean that the trial examiner, like the early English equity judge, would be required only to see that the policies of the Act were effected and would need little regard for seeming consistency or prior precedent. Because this context has not been followed, one of the more widely quoted criticisms of the NLRB is that it has not given sufficient attention to the differing impact upon employees of what objectively is the same employer conduct. In other words, the same action taken with regard to truck drivers in Detroit or textile mill employees in the South may result in one group being coerced and the other group not being coerced. This attitude has also led others to suggest special legislation for particular groups. This in part was accomplished for the apparel and construction industries in the 1959 amendments. This problem would not exist (though others might) if the Board paid more attention to "justice" and less to precedent.

Unfortunately, the trend has been toward increasing legalism and the drawing of fine lines which exclude or include a particular course of conduct. A similar tendency is noticeable in all federal agencies and even in some private areas like arbitration, which may only indicate that it is a product of our complex age. More likely, the trend toward increased legalism is a search for a seeming consistency or certainty which some always seem to find in the application of specific rules of behavior as opposed to rules concerning the impact of that behavior upon other parties. Modern-day critics of the Board's decisions, who see a pressing need for certainty of result, and who argue that employers must know as precisely as possible what they can say to their employees, might well quote the author of *A Replication of a Sergeante at the Lawes of England* (c. 1530), who in protesting the Chancellor's interference with the due course of the law, said:

Conscience is a thing of great uncertaintie, for some men thinke that if they treade upon two straws that lie across, that they offend in conscience, and some men thinketh that if he take money, and another hath too moche, he may take part of his with conscience; and so, diverse men, diverse consciences.[13]

Labor policy is also affected by the decisions of Circuit Courts of Appeals to which cases may be taken by aggrieved parties to Board decisions or by the Board if it does not receive voluntary compliance with its orders. The circuit courts do not retry the cases, but may rule upon points of law and upon whether the factual record as a whole that was before the Board supports its determination. Beyond the circuit courts lies the Supreme Court.

Cases follow three routes to the Supreme Court. A few, like the

[13] Taken from Sir Charles Ogilvie, *King's Government and Common Law 1471–1641*, Oxford: Basil Blackwell, 1958, p. 30.

suit between California and Arizona over the Colorado River water, come under the Court's original jurisdiction. A second group consists of those which are appealed from the decisions of a lower court. These cases involve decisions in which: (1) some act has been declared unconstitutional; (2) a state court has made a decision based upon a federal law; and (3) the question concerns the validity of a state law when viewed in the light of the federal constitution. The Supreme Court has held that union-management relations of local business affecting interstate commerce are governed by federal law; thus, a state court decision applying state law to such a situation can be appealed to the Supreme Court. Certiorari covers the remainder of the cases. It is essentially a request that the Court decide the case. About 1000 petitions for certiorari a year are received by the Court and approximately 90 percent of all these petitions are refused, rarely with any explanation being given for the action. This does not mean, as justices have often written, that the Supreme Court approves or disapproves of the outcome in the lower courts. It only means that at least four justices did not find that the case warranted a decision by the Supreme Court. The two principal reasons for granting certiorari are: (1) where there are divergent decisions among the circuit courts in similar cases; and (2) where the case raises important issues for the first time. Once the writ has been granted, the case is decided by the Court, either by a signed opinion, or by a *per curiam* (for the Court) opinion which usually merely reverses or affirms the decision of the next lower court. In a few rare cases the Court will conclude that certiorari was improvidently granted, no formal decision will be made, and the circuit court's decision governs the case.

INTERPRETING THE LAW

After the Supreme Court takes a case, upon what is its formal opinion based? The law, of course, but what is the law? Is it Iolanthe's "The law is the true embodiment of everything that is excellent," or Mr. Justice Holmes's, "The prophecies of what the courts will do in fact, and nothing more pretentious, are what I mean by law"?

For most labor cases, stemming as they do from specific legislation by Congress, the reference is to what Congress said, or in the more expressive words of Justice Frankfurter:

> The judicial function is confined to applying what Congress enacted after ascertaining what it is that Congress enacted. But such ascertainment, that is construing legislation, is nothing like a mechanical endeavor. It could not be accomplished by the subtlest of modern "brain" machines. Because of the infirmities of language and the limited scope of science in legislative drafting, inevitably there enters into the construction of statutes the play of judicial judgment within the limits of the relevant legislative materials. Most relevant, of course, is the very language in which Congress has expressed its policy and from which the Court must extract the meaning most appropriate.[14]

In some instances this will mean the use of the exact words, even though these may do violence to what may have seemed the clear intent of Congress when it used the words. A possible example is the Taft-Hartley Act's abortive attempt to outlaw featherbedding. The wording of Section 8 (b) (6) was to make it an unfair labor practice "to cause or attempt to cause an employer to pay or deliver or agree to pay or deliver any money or other thing of value in the nature of an exaction for services which are not performed or not to be performed." Since the section was passed in a period when it had become apparent that the Lea (Anti-Petrillo) Act would come to naught, it might be reasonable to assume that the new section was designed to at least deal with the activities of the Musicians Union. Heretofore this union had required that whenever a traveling group of musicians was playing in an area a standby orchestra of local men had to be hired. This was clearly illegal under 8 (b) (6), so the union merely indicated that the

[14] *Local 1976 Carpenters Union* v. NLRB, 357 U.S. 93 at 100 (1957); 42 LRRM 2243 at 2266.

local musicians would play during periods when the audience was
moving into and out of their seats. This was a useless gesture in
the eyes of management. Yet in *NLRB* v. *Gamble Enterprises*[15]
the Supreme Court upheld the legality of the new arrangement
because some services were provided. In that decision, and in its
companion, *NLRB* v. *American Newspaper Publishers Association*,[16] where the legality of setting bogus type was upheld upon
a similar reading of the definition of the word services, can be
seen one of the clearest infirmities of language—the multiple
meaning of words. Did the word "services" mean *any* service or
only those which an employer wished to have performed?

The problem of multiple meanings is somewhat clearer when
the word has both general and technical meanings. Then the
question is which meaning Congress had in mind when it wrote
the legislation. One of the least useful aspects of the original
Taft-Hartley Act was the requirement that in order to utilize
the services of the Board, there had to be:

. . . on file with the Board an affidavit executed contemporaneously
or within the preceding twelve-month period by each officer of such
labor organization and the officers of any national or international
labor organization of which it is an affiliate or constituent unit that he
is not a member of the Communist Party or affiliated with such party,
and that he does not believe in, and is not a member of or supports
any organization that believes in or teaches the overthrow of the United
States Government by force or by any illegal or unconstitutional
methods.

In two separate cases the Supreme Court was called upon to
define the words "international labor organization" and "officer."
In both instances, the common meaning won out over the technical. In one, the Congress of Industrial Organization was declared an international labor organization despite the fact that
that word would not be used in professional circles to describe

[15] *NLRB* v. *Gamble Enterprises*, 345 U.S. 17 (1953); 31 LRRM 2428.
[16] *NLRB* v. *American Newspaper Publishers Association*, 345 U.S. 100
(1953); 31 LRRM 2422.

the CIO. In the other case, the Court held that the NLRB had acted reasonably in defining officers to mean constitutional ones, and thus an international representative was merely an agent, not an officer.

There are times when the words are not enough or when different parts of the same legislation seem to imply different results. In *NLRB* v. *Teamsters*[17] the Court held that, while Congress had not made the right to strike an absolute one, any and all restrictions were always narrowly and explicitly set out. Thus it was incorrect for the Labor Board to try to broaden the restrictions. And in the recent *Erie Resistor*[18] case, where the company had granted strike replacements 20 years of seniority to protect them from the problem of layoffs (it then required 8 years of seniority to hold one's job), the Court felt constrained to weigh the rights granted to the employees to strike against those of the employer to replace, and concluded that, in this instance, the right to replace had to be subjugated to the right to strike. A similar balancing problem between rights of employees and rights of employers has been required when the question of lockouts has been considered.

There will be times, however, when reference to words, congressional style, etc., will be found wanting and recourse will be made to the intent of the legislature. An appeal to the intent of the legislature rather than directly to the words of the statute is a common one, but one fraught with certain difficulties. Indeed, many years ago the Supreme Court did not do it.

In construing an Act of Congress, we are not at liberty to recur to the views of individual members in debate nor to consider the motives which influenced them to vote for or against passage. The Act itself speaks the will of Congress and this is to be ascertained from the language used.[19]

[17] *NLRB* v. *Drivers, Chauffeurs, Helpers, Local Union No. 639*, 362 U.S. 274 (1960).
[18] *NLRB* v. *Erie Resistor Corp.*, 373 U.S. 221 (1963); 53 LRRM 2121.
[19] *United States* v. *Union Pacific Railroad*, 91 U.S. 72 at 79 (1875).

Over the years a more flexible standard has evolved which allows recourse to various measures of legislative intent. If the Court is to put itself into the position of those who wrote the legislation, to what should they look? Some of the places would be the reports of the committees, the statements of legislators, especially if they play a leading role in the passage of a particular bill or if they are the leaders of the opposition. There are obvious difficulties with this approach. Too little emphasis may be placed upon the context in which an answer is given, or one answer may be cited in preference to a different one to the same or a similar question. A suggestion as to how an act should be interpreted may even be manufactured for the legislative record and not because there is widespread agreement upon the exact outcome. In fact, one or two individuals may be able to secure a specific result through a Court interpretation of their remarks that would have been impossible in the form of an amendment.

For constitutional questions somewhat broader rules of construction are allowed. This more liberal interpretation is usually explained by reference to the fact that the legislature can, if it does not like a line of interpretation, rewrite the law, whereas this is not so easily done for the Constitution. Of the two basic approaches to constitutional interpretation, one has been well set out by Justice Sutherland in *Home Building and Loan Association* v. *Blaisdell*:[20]

The whole aim of construction as applied to a provision of the Constitution is to discover the meaning, to ascertain and give effect to the intent of its framers and the people who adopted it. . . . As nearly as possible we should place ourselves in the condition of those who framed and adopted it.

The other approach seeks to take the spirit of the framers and apply it to the situation of the moment. It was well presented by Justice Holmes in *Missouri* v. *Holland*.[21]

[20] *Home Building and Loan Association* v. *Blaisdell*, 290 U.S. 398 (1934).
[21] *Missouri* v. *Holland*, 252 U.S. 416 (1920) at 433.

. . . When we are dealing with words that also are a constituent act, like the Constitution of the United States, we must realize that they have called into life a being the development of which could not have been foreseen completely by the most gifted of its begetters. It was enough for them to realize or to hope that they had created an organism; it has taken a century and has cost their successors much sweat and blood to prove that they created a nation. The case before us must be considered in the light of our whole experience and not merely in that of what was said a hundred years ago.

It should now be clear that courts are not merely setting down the course of action next to the statute to see if one fits the other. Rather, each court is legislating, filling in the open gaps in the law, although in most cases the judge operates within narrow limits. Judges thus play an active, rather than a passive role and "judge-made law" is a fact and not to be deplored except when it exceeds certain ill-defined limits.

FACTS AND LAWS

So far we have discussed cases purely in terms of legal rules but these rules are evolved in particular cases which also involve facts. And the facts may be as important or more important than the legal rule. Justice Jerome Frank told of one of his early cases where the judge, after giving the opposing party the benefit of every doubt concerning the admission or exclusion of evidence, decided, with strong findings of fact, in favor of Frank's client.[22] Some years later the judge explained to Justice Frank that he felt "justice" to be with Frank's party and an "unjust" legal rule to favor the opposition. His conduct precluded reversal, for all of the legal points favored the loser and facts determined by a lower court or administrative agency are seldom overruled.

Facts in labor cases present two types of problems. One is the

[22] The story is told in Jerome Frank, "Words and Music: Some Remarks on Statutory Interpretation," *Columbia Law Review*, 47, December 1947, pp. 1260–1278.

truth or falsity of a specific claim. This point is well-illustrated in the *Mount Hope Finishing Company*[23] case, the first one involving a run-away shop charge. The Northern textile industry was suffering a severe depression and the plant was operating at less than one-half capacity with a three- and four-day work week. Suddenly the company was faced with the signed union cards of a majority of its employees and a demand that the union be recognized. The company refused this demand without an NLRB election. A strike ensued during which the company continued to operate. In the context of that emotional scene two statements were made. In a speech to the striking workers, the aged president of the family firm said, according to the union, that there would always be a Mount Hope Company in North Dighton, Massachusetts. He claimed to have said only that he would never leave North Dighton. In the second instance the company treasurer was quoted as saying that the mill was closing because of the advent of the union, but the treasurer insisted that he said only that the mill was closing because of economic conditions which the union had only heightened.

Of perhaps greater importance is what agreed-upon facts mean. In *Mount Hope*, one of the questions raised was whether any attempt had been made to obtain new business for the "temporarily" closed Massachusetts plant (it never reopened). Management's spokesman replied yes, and he listed several firms whom he had contacted. True, replied the government, but for the largest nonintegrated finishing plant in the industry, these contacts represented no real effort, for they could not generate sufficient business to keep the plant running.

Similarly, there is the question of whether certain facts fit particular legal rules. This can be seen in a controversy among members of the Board in 1962–1963 over one appropriate unit for bargaining. A union of insurance agents asked for a unit composed of all of one class of employees whose offices were within

[23] *Mount Hope Finishing Co.*, 106 NLRB 480 (1953); 32 LRRM 1492; set aside 211 F. 2d 365 (1954), 33 LRRM 2742.

the city of Chicago. This request was turned down by the regional director because some city agents covered territories outside the city limits while outside agents also worked within the city. The director found a metropolitan area unit to be the appropriate one. The Board (3–2) overruled him. The Chicago city limits which the union had asked, were allowed on the rationale that the companies' administrative lines covering territories might be redrawn at any time, while an office was either in or out of the city of Chicago, the geographical boundaries of which were quite stable. The dissenters on the Board said the sole reason for the city rather than the metropolitan area was that the city offices were those where they had organized and that the use of "union organization" as a criterion had been forbidden by the 1947 statute. But, said the majority, we have indicated our sound reasons for our choice of unit and "extent of organization" is not one of them. All of which seems to imply that something is what it is called.

Before one concludes that the law is like Alice's wonderland, where things become what they are called, it is well to recognize that these are but manifestations of the general problem of how to treat equally those things which are equals. Whenever two things have more than one facet, equal treatment on the basis of one will probably mean discrimination in terms of others. Examples abound in all aspects of life. The relevant question then becomes, not whether equals have been treated equally, but whether the test for equality is a reasonable one. Viewed in this manner, it is doubtful whether the law is any more inconsistent and unfair than are other areas of life.

SUGGESTED READINGS

LOREN P. BETH, *Politics, the Constitution and the Supreme Court,* New York: Harper & Row, 1962.

BENJAMIN N. CARDOZO, *The Nature of the Judicial Process*, New Haven: Yale University Press, 1921.

OLIVER WENDELL HOLMES, JR., *The Common Law*, Boston: Little, Brown, 1881.

ROBERT C. McCLOSKEY, *The American Supreme Court*, Chicago: University of Chicago Press, 1960.

CHAPTER 4

The Legislative History
and Theory of
Federal Statute Labor Policy

LEGISLATIVE HISTORY

An understanding of current labor laws will be enhanced by some appreciation of the process by which they evolved and a knowledge of some of the factors which have been important in their passage. Statutory federal labor policy, defined as laws with a significant impact upon unions and their activities, begins with the passage of the Interstate Commerce Act in 1877. Its effect was primarily upon railroad unions, a group with which this book does not deal because federal policy has been separately determined for these unions since World War I. The impact of this law upon unions was unexpected. It arose when the courts decided that the antidiscrimination provisions of the Act, designed to police the rate-setting ability of the railroads, also prevented engineers on one railroad from refusing to handle cars of a road with whom their fellow unionists had a dispute.

Sherman Act

The next expression of congressional policy, the Sherman Anti-trust law of 1890, was also not primarily intended to regulate unions. And, like the Interstate Commerce Act, its application to union activity may have been unforeseen and unintended by the legislature. The effect upon labor that Congress expected when it passed the Sherman Act has been subject to widespread debate and forms an interesting chapter in the role of the intent of Congress in determining the future course of governmental policy. Senator George F. Edmunds, probably the chief draftsman of the law, said in an 1892 interview, "I think it will cover every form of combination—whether it be capital . . . or labor. . . ."[1] Other observers gathered a different impression from various members of the legislature; among these were Samuel Gompers and Commissioner Lennon of the United States Commission on Industrial Relations. The Supreme Court, when called upon to decide this question in *Loewe* v. *Lawlor*[2] (Danbury Hatters, 1908), held that Congress had intended to include unions since efforts had been made during its passage to exclude labor, but that the exclusion had not been extended to the final law. Those who feel Congress did not intend such a result argue that the Court misread the context within which the labor exceptions were offered.

Briefly, the labor exemptions arose in the context of discussions concerning the prohibition of combinations of individuals or groups which tended to raise prices to consumers. This was consistent with earlier legislation against trusts which mentioned rising prices and excluded farmers and laborers. When the wording of the bill was changed to cover combinations in restraint of trade, the labor exemptions were dropped. The determination of whether the labor and farmer exemptions applied to the concept of anti-trust or only to the test of rising prices is not clear and is probably

---

[1] From Edward Berman, *Labor and the Sherman Act*, New York: Harper & Row, 1930, p. 6.

[2] *Loewe* v. *Lawlor*, 208 U.S. 274 (1908).

of limited and only historical interest. Regardless of intent, the law was applied to labor. About 90 percent of all cases which were handled under the Sherman Act from its passage to 1897 dealt with labor, and between 1890 and 1928 about 18 percent of all cases involved Sherman Act applications to labor organizations.

Clayton Act

Unions made extensive efforts to eliminate their activities from the control of the Sherman Act. The 1908 and 1912 platforms of the Democratic party included provisions favoring the exclusion of labor from the Sherman Act and limitation of the use of injunctions. The liberal wing of the Republican party was unable to secure the inclusion of similar proposals in its party's platforms.

The inclusion of a proposal to exclude labor from anti-trust laws in Democratic platforms did not assure its enactment when the party gained control of the government. President Wilson, partly because his "new freedom" was opposed to class legislation, and perhaps because he hadn't accepted the American Federation of Labor as a worthwhile institution, did not agree with the presidential platform of his party and was opposed to and did not include a labor provision in his early anti-trust proposals. Then in 1914, the President proposed to include language saying that the Sherman Act did not forbid unions. This action was taken because he felt a growing need for increased labor support, and because there was pressure from congressmen up for re-election. In a practical sense, all that would have been accomplished would have been to give federal statutory sanction to what had been judicially noted in Judge Shaw's famous decision in *Commonwealth* v. *Hunt*[3] in 1842—namely, that the labor union in and of itself was not illegal.

At first labor was happy with the provision. Then the AFL wanted the provision changed to read "does not apply to unions," but the President refused to support this. In due time the last line of Section 6 of the Clayton Act was adopted. This said, in

[3] *Commonwealth* v. *Hunt*, 4 Metcalf 111 (Mass., 1842).

essence, that unions were not illegal combinations or conspiracies in restraint of trade under the anti-trust laws. The wording was hailed by supporters of labor as breaking the bonds which had bound unions. Within the Congress the results were less clear. The Chairman of the House Rules Committee said that the section had taken labor out from under the Sherman Act, but the Chairman of the Judicial Committee felt that the original concept, that of merely affirming the legality of union organization, was all the section contained.

This dispute over congressional intent was settled by the Supreme Court. In *Duplex* v. *Deering*[4] (1921), the Court declared that no real change in the position of unions under the anti-trust laws had been accomplished in the Clayton Act. Almost 20 years later new life was given to the Clayton Act by Justice Frankfurter in the 1940 Hutcheson decision, but by then the whole of labor-management relations had changed.

Norris-LaGuardia Act

Regardless of the legal accuracy of the Court's 1921 Duplex decision concerning the congressional intent, it probably expressed the mood of the majority of the populace. The 1920s was the era of the *open shop* movement and consequently the role and influence of unions decreased. One of the weapons utilized in the campaign against unions was the injunction. An injunction is a legal order which can be obtained from an equity court in order to restrain activities which would cause irreparable harm to property. Thus, an injunction could not be obtained to prevent someone from building a fence on disputed property, for if the builder were incorrect, monetary damages would ease the harm. An injunction could be obtained to prevent an old and valuable tree from being cut down in order to build the fence, for money could not compensate for the loss of the tree. In the context of union activities, injunctions were secured primarily to prevent damage to the intangible property associated with the firm's right to conduct busi-

[4] *Duplex Printing Press Co.* v. *Deering*, 254 U.S. 443 (1921).

ness. Used alone it may not have been terribly effective, but in combination with the yellow-dog contract, it was a much more potent weapon, for only then could it be used by a firm to prevent its own workers from joining unions if they so chose. Nowhere was this combination used more actively and perhaps more effectively than in the coal fields.

Congressional efforts were made over a number of years by friends of labor to restrict the use of injunctions. These efforts to remove the millstone of the injunction at the federal level began when Senator Shipstead of Minnesota introduced, for his friend Andrew Furuseth, President of the International Seamen's Union, a law which would allow injunctions to protect only property which was tangible and transferable. This excluded the intangible and largely nontransferable business relationships which was what the labor injunctions sought to protect. Hearings on the bill did not reveal a great deal of support, and even unions felt it would be ineffective and unworkable. At the conclusion of the hearings a group of men met with Senator Norris of Nebraska and drafted a new bill aimed at the same purpose, a draft which would become law many months later. In the 1928 election campaign, Hoover favored curbing abuses in the use of injunctions, while Al Smith's platform favored curbing their use. The AFL attempted to make the injunction a major issue in the campaign, but met with no great success. By October of 1929 the AFL had given its support to the Norris bill. Its earlier failure to do so was based upon support for Furuseth and the AFL's desire to include amendments making jurisdictional and consumer boycotts legal. Norris and his supporters felt that these amendments would be like red flags in the bull ring to many congressmen.

Debates over the approval of several judicial appointments were utilized to dramatize the situation. Within Congress, the bill was still in committee and the observable efforts seemed aimed at preventing the appointments of Charles Evans Hughes and John J. Parker to the Supreme Court. Hughes was attacked as the representative of powerful interests, but won confirmation 52 to 26.

Parker, opposed by the NAACP for some remarks concerning
Negroes, the United Mine Workers for his Red Jacket decision
(a blanket injunction), and the AFL, was defeated. In the past
50 years, he is the only man who holds this distinction. With the
1930 elections producing a Democratic victory in the House and
a drastic reduction in the Republicans' Senate majority, prospects
for the measure appeared to brighten. In December of 1931 the
AFL gave up its last proposed amendments and offered its unqualified support to the Norris proposal. The states of New York,
Pennsylvania, Wisconsin, and Ohio passed similar measures. Then
on January 12, 1932, President Hoover named District Judge J. H.
(Injunction Judge) Wilkerson to the Seventh Circuit Court of
Appeals. Fifteen days later at the height of the outcry against
Wilkerson's appointment, Norris's bill was reported out of com-
mittee 11 to 5. On March 1, 1932, the Senate passed it 75 to 5
and eight days later the House followed by a 362 to 14 vote. The
President, without clarifying his position, quietly signed it on
March 23, 1932. Then, six years later, the Supreme Court accepted
its constitutionality. Despite its subsequent major role in policy,
it was a quiet victory, appearing on page 34 of the *New York
Times*, while the April *American Federationist* did little more
than summarize it.

Wagner Act

The depression not only helped to pass the Norris-LaGuardia
Act, but it also played a commanding role in the development of
the Wagner Act. In March of 1933, Senator Wagner of New
York had been asked by Roosevelt to shape legislative planning
for recovery measures. In April, Raymond Moley, who headed
Roosevelt's "Brain Trust," was also asked to work on such a
measure. Moley and General Hugh Johnson, who was to be the
first administrator of the National Industrial Recovery Board,
were not too interested in anything for labor, but the political
role of the AFL in support of Senator Black's 30-hour law suggested that perhaps some balancing feature for labor should be

added. Out of this concern came Section 7a of the National
Industrial Recovery Act. It provided that workers should have
the right to "organize and bargain collectively through representatives of their own choosing, and shall be free from interference,
restraint, or coercion of employers . . . in the designation of such
representatives or in self organization. . . ." In the House the
section occasioned no great mention and even the Chamber of
Commerce favored it, though not the National Association of
Manufacturers.

In the Senate hearings the NAM position became much stronger.
Their concern was not with the idea of unions, but with outside
unionism, where employees of more than one firm belonged to
the same union, though many would not recognize NAM-favored
employee representation as unionism. It was as Mr. Dooley said
13 years earlier, " 'Shure,' said Mr. Dooley, 'if properly conducted.
An' there we are: an' how would they have them [unions] conducted? No strikes, no rules, no contracts, no scales, hardly iny
wages, an' dam' few mimbers.' "[5]

The value of Section 7a for organized labor was slight. On
behalf of outside unionism there was, with the exception of John
L. Lewis, David Dubinsky, and Sidney Hillman, little attempt to
take advantage of the provisions of 7a. Many companies, however, set up house unions and by 1935 there were perhaps as many
captive as outside union members. In August of 1933 the National
Labor Board chaired by Senator Wagner was set up as called for
by the Act. It had a vague mandate, undefined procedures, and
no direct power of enforcement. The National Labor Board did
contribute to the development of policy, particularly to the idea
of an election of one agent as sole representative, with the implied
concept of a single union based upon majority choice, as opposed
to multiple representation by local unions each representing only
its own members. Three months after the Board's founding,

[5] From Finley Peter Dunne, "Mr. Dooley on The Open Shop," *Literary
Digest*, November 27, 1920.

companies began to ignore it and by February of the following year, its usefulness had ended.

There was an attempt to revive the Board, but it was half-hearted at best. An executive order designed to strengthen the Board was issued and an unofficial comment that the government ought to check the growth of company unions was issued by President Roosevelt. Two days later, however, Hugh Johnson and Donald Richberg, Johnson's deputy and later chairman of the National Industrial Recovery Board, spoke in favor of multiple representation as opposed to the exclusive representation of the National Labor Board. Then in the following month, the President became publicly associated with multiple representation in the famous Auto code case. This was a situation where a combination of: (1) industry indifference to the National Recovery Administration; (2) very limited AFL support among the workers; and (3) a government very desirous of having the automobile industry's cooperation resulted in the bulk of management's views being incorporated into the labor provisions of the code for that industry. Included in the labor codes was the concept of multiple representation, which to organized labor meant company unions.

Prior to the complete demise of the National Labor Board, Senator Wagner had become convinced that something outside of the National Recovery Act was needed for labor. He and several associates drafted a bill which he introduced in March of 1934. This time the protests of business were more audible and President Roosevelt, still hoping for industry support for NRA, declined to give it his support. Emerging as a compromise was Public Resolution 44 of June of 1934. The NLRB, established under Public Resolution 44, could hold elections, demand company payrolls, and was free of the NRA. It also included exclusive as opposed to multiple representation—but it had no power. Between July 1, 1934 and March 1, 1935 there were 33 noncompliance cases and no court judgments.

The 1934 election strengthened the Democrats, and in the

following year Senator Wagner again introduced his bill. The President again held back. Secretary of Labor Frances Perkins described the bill as "very interesting," Donald Richberg was opposed, and the *Boston Herald* called it a "closed shop" bill. Roosevelt's position was not surprising. Labor was not his field of primary experience or clear-cut views, and while there was some sympathy for the idea of labor as a counterweight to industry, it was not a well-developed concept. Factory legislation would have been much closer to his view of a measure to assist the working man. Nor was he alone; Wagner was one of very few liberal Democrats who placed a high value upon trade unions. Organized industry took its expected stand, as the *Commercial and Financial Chronicle* said, "It was one of the most objectionable, as well as one of the most revolutionary pieces of legislation ever presented to Congress."

The opposition, however, had little effect. The bill was reported out of the Senate Committee on May 2, 1935, brought onto the floor on the 15th, and passed 63–12 on the following day. In the House there was real support and the bill passed easily. Whether support for Wagner's bill was because of the strength of the labor lobby, or because it was a high point of the New Deal, or the expectation that the Supreme Court would invalidate the entire bill is not clear. If passage of the bill had in fact depended upon the Supreme Court's expected refusal to allow it, those congressmen who voted in favor of it were disappointed, since the Court failed to play its expected role and upheld the legality of the Wagner Act in the *Jones & Laughlin Steel Corp.*[6] case in 1937.

Taft-Hartley Act

When the Supreme Court failed them, opponents of the Wagner Act concepts turned again to the legislature. In the next 10 years, although 169 amendments were offered, most did not receive formal consideration and none came close to being passed.

[6] *NLRB* v. *Jones & Laughlin Steel Corp.*, 301 U.S. 1 (1937); 1 LRRM 703.

It was not until the rise of the Congress of Industrial Organization and World War II had changed the context of industrial relations sufficiently so that the Wagner Act was no longer regarded as untouchable, that basic amendments became possible. This, combined with the method of financing World War II which delayed the inflation until after the war and allowed unions to unjustifiably absorb much of the blame for rising prices, and some legitimate complaints over certain unions' activities, set the stage for reform.

A number of individuals and groups were interested in sponsoring amendments. President Truman asked Congress for a bill outlawing jurisdictional and secondary boycott strikes and requiring the final arbitration of grievances. The more conservative-minded members of Congress had much more repressive ideas in mind. An observer might have predicted a relatively mild bill, because the electorate probably required some measure, the President supported limited reform, and the extreme reformers and the staunch supporters of unions would tend to cancel one another's efforts. Organized labor was partly responsible for the results. Its members' refusal to suggest any positive legislative proposals irritated sympathetic members of Congress. Perhaps a more important reason was the commanding role of Senator Taft who fought off reactionary members of his own party as fiercely as he did the liberal Democrats.

The Taft-Hartley Act emerged from Congress, was vetoed by President Truman, and then passed over his veto. When compared to the Wagner Act, the Taft-Hartley Act, at least in its written form, was a rather drastic reorientation of legislative policy. As a result, it became a major issue in the presidential campaign of 1948. Mr. Truman's surprise victory in that election caused a number of liberals and labor leaders to expect that there would be major changes in the Taft-Hartley bill. One otherwise perceptive academic student of labor-management affairs even went so far as to write an article in which he stated that he wished to assess the impact of the Taft-Hartley Act before many of its provisions were amended.

Efforts to amend the new labor law were unsuccessful. The fact that they were of no avail rests, in part, with the unions themselves. Their position was not a united one. The Railroad Brotherhoods, the United Mine Workers, the AFL, and the CIO were at odds over various aspects of the Act. Of greater importance was union insistence on a complete repeal of the Taft-Hartley Act to be followed later in the congressional term by a separate bill which would amend the Wagner Act. Unions were also opposed to the use of injunctions in cases of national emergency disputes. Complete repeal and then amendment was unacceptable to the Congress and failure to provide some measure to deal with emergency disputes was unacceptable to the administration. The result was no legislation. Though it may appear that, had the unions been able to agree among themselves, and had they been willing to rid the Taft-Hartley law of only those features which they found most objectionable instead of pressing to eliminate every section which was displeasing to them, those desiring amendment would have met with success. There were, however, other factors at work which were not so favorable to change. Of those members of Congress who voted to override President Truman's veto, 54 were still in the Senate and 226 in the House. Also, much of the Democratic strength was from southern states and these men were little influenced by union or labor pressure. Also, the administration needed the southerners' support for other measures and could apply only limited pressure to obtain new labor legislation.

Unions and their political allies continued to press for a reversal of the Taft-Hartley law, but as the years passed the opportunities for success became smaller and smaller. There were several reasons for this. One was the inability of unions, despite major effort, to defeat their self-selected arch foe, Senator Taft, in his bid for re-election in 1950. A second was the fact that experience under the Taft-Hartley Act proved to be far less harmful to unions than might have been expected from its literal wording. A good example of this is in the provisions which allowed unions to be sued for damages. The unions talked of management efforts to destroy them through excessive judgments. Few unions have been sued, for the facts of the industrial world are such that even a successful suit against a union is apt to be a poor policy in most instances. But perhaps the most important reason there were no major amendments to the Taft-Hartley Act was the continued domination of Congress by a combination of Republicans and southern Democrats similar to those who had passed the initial legislation.

FEDERAL STATUTE LABOR POLICY

The basic outlines of this country's development of a public policy toward labor are well known but the various factors which underlie its particular course are not so clear. Consequently, a simple theory which can encompass the historical twists and turns, as well as provide refutable hypotheses concerning the course of future events, has not emerged. One reason for this is a result of a tendency to consider the largely judicial policy of the nineteenth century and the largely statute policy of the twentieth century as a single whole to be explained by the same variables and forces. It is not clear, however, that the isolated court cases which make up nineteenth-century policy are the result of consistent choices. After all, these were state courts, and even today states vary widely in their policies. A good example is provided by *Plant* v. *Woods*[7] (1900) and *National Protective Association* v. *Cumming*[8] (1902). Only two years and a common geographical boundary separated the highest courts of Massachusetts and New York, yet in dealing with strikes to enforce closed shop provisions, one wrote in *Plant* v. *Woods* (1900):

Such acts [the threat of a union to strike to enforce a closed shop] are without justification, and therefore are malicious and unlawful. . . .

[7] *Plant* v. *Woods*, 176 Mass. 492 (1900) at 502.
[8] *National Protective Association* v. *Cumming*, 170 N.Y. 315 (1902) at 321.

while the other said in *National Protective Association* v. *Cumming* (1902):

> The reason [a union decides to strike] may no more be demanded as a right, of organization than of an individual, but if they elect to state their reason their right to stop work is not cut off because the reason seems inadequate or selfish to the employer or organized society.

Another difficulty stems from viewing policy as having gradually evolved from an overemphasis upon the rights of property, and consequently becoming more favorable to management to a point where increased emphasis was put upon individual or minority rights, and thus became more favorable to unions. Such a view is favored through the passage of the Wagner Act, but is unable to explain the regression to the Taft-Hartley Act. A successful theory would be more apt to concentrate upon statute policy and would allow for alternating shifts in policies favorable to unions.

The Theory

The concept of the public interest which was suggested in Chapter 2 provides an important clue to an appropriate theory. We defined public interest as the requirement of a dominant consensus regarding the rules of the game and their amendment, but only a simple majority to determine the particular value of any rule at any given moment. Since specific private interests are typically at variance with those of most other individuals and groups, it is to be expected that even simple majority consensus on any single issue may be difficult to achieve most of the time. Thus, policy on many matters may be one of default rather than of conscious choice. In other words, at a point in time a majority consensus is obtained and legislation is passed. Subsequently, even though the results of applying that piece of legislation may no longer be in accord with what the majority favors, government agencies will continue to apply it in the old way because the costs of obtaining a new consensus and new legislation are greater than the interested parties are willing to pay. For example, it is quite probable that the Taft-Hartley Act could have been amended in 1949 in return for a major weakening in the coverage and benefit level of Social Security, Workman's Compensation, etc. Viewed in this manner, the expectation is that public policy toward labor, especially union organization, would be a product of the general consensus of the period upon national goals, desirable organizations, and accidental factors, and it would not represent specific conscious policy until the situation was one of concern to a large number of individuals or to those with political power.

The Theory and Its Application

The briefest survey of labor history would indicate that the union movement was never numerically important until after the depression of the early 1930s. This was partly due to the abhorrence with which it was viewed by employers and their consequent efforts to combat its growth. "A worker today, a capitalist tomorrow" feeling is often said to have characterized the majority of the work force in the nineteenth century. There was also the probable basic distrust of unionism by the American people—not a surprising attitude considering union intoleration toward immigrants, women, Chinese, and Negroes. This is not the place to investigate nonpolicy factors in union growth, but a recognition of organized labor's almost complete inability to attract members, other than in a few occupations and industries, is necessary to an understanding of policy development. Considering the above, the pre-1937 definition of the commerce clause of the Constitution to mean the actual flow of goods between states and the belief that the less public regulation of business, the better, it is not surprising to find that most of the time public policy treated unions as if they were businesses. Unions are not firms, and a legal framework designed to regulate business tended to hobble the effectiveness of unions except in those brief periods when they were favored by the economic tides of the period.

The two pieces of nineteenth-century federal legislation which affected union labor, the Interstate Commerce Act and the Sherman Act, fit nicely into this framework. The impact of the first was clearly unintended and can be explained as the accidental product of public officials applying the rules at hand to a new situation. Within the legislature, concern for the union position was not sufficient to amend the Interstate Commerce Act to preclude a similar decision in subsequent circumstances. When the Sherman Act was being debated in Congress and there was the possibility that it might impede any activity of *workers* which tended to raise wages, there was enough sentiment to foreclose such a result. When the wording was changed to cover combinations in restraint of trade, congressional concern with organized labor was seemingly insufficient to obtain a proviso excluding unions. Why there was concern with workers as opposed to unions is difficult to say. A possible explanation would be that the initial exclusion was obtained only because it was also necessary to provide an exclusion for any actions of farmers which raised prices. The failure of any union exclusion provision in the final bill would then stem from the lack of support by agricultural legislators.

As one author has termed it, the Clayton Act is an enigma. On the surface, and as seen by some of those who passed upon it, it conferred upon organized labor the benefits which it had sought since the true character of the Sherman Act as related to unions became known through the action of the Courts. In this light the Clayton Act would deserve Gompers' ringing statement:

> In no other country in the world is there an enunciation of fundamental principle comparable to the incisive, virile statement in section 6. . . . The declaratory legislation 'the labor of a human being is not a commodity or article of commerce,' is the industrial Magna Charta upon which the working people will rear their structure of industrial freedom.[9]

The Supreme Court read the Act differently, seeing nothing but President Wilson's stated desire to make clear unions' freedom to use legal means to organize. Clearly, the sympathy of the admin-

[9] From *American Federationist*, November, 1914.

istration and the liberalism of the progressive movement were not enough to produce a law unambiguously favorable to organized labor. On other labor issues there was more success. A child labor law, subsequently declared unconstitutional (5–4) by the Supreme Court, and a workmen's compensation act for federal employees were enacted during Wilson's administration. Seemingly, the appropriate conclusion is that the consensus of the day was a concern for workers, but not for organized workers.

The only possible flaw in the argument given above was the passage in 1915 of the Seamen's Acts whose express purpose was the raising of wages and the securing of jobs for American seamen. A major beneficiary of the law was the seamen's union. Yet this measure was not as inconsistent as it may seem. Its impact was only upon a very small portion of business and most of its clauses could be justified by reference to safety at sea, matters of no small concern following the loss of the *Titanic* in 1912 with 1500 lives and the *Volturno* which burned at sea on October 11, 1913 with the loss of over 200 lives. More important, the exclusion of oriental competition by a requirement that the seamen be able to understand the language of their officers found support from labor, certain western interests, and southerners who favored any kind of white supremacy. The hope given for the revival of American flag shipping upon the international waters delighted the imperialists and perhaps made some sense in a world torn by war. And lastly it drew to it the humanitarians interested in justice for the seamen and safety at sea. Thus, it is doubtful that success would have been achieved on the labor issue of higher wages and more jobs alone. As a matter of fact, the manner in which the Act was administered by the Commerce Department made many of its seeming advances meaningless and World War I did far more for the economic position of the seamen and the strength of their union than did the provisions of the Seamen's Acts.

With the end of World War I, the red scare, Warren G. Harding, and the Open Shop drive, the probability of favorable labor legislation was small. The decline in organized membership from some 5 million at the end of World War I to 3.4 million in 1930 (due largely to the decline of wartime industries and the depression in the coal and apparel trades) only lessened the probability. The fact that a majority consensus for favorable legislation was reached in the passage of the Norris-LaGuardia Act can probably best be explained by: (1) the onset of the depression; (2) a union willingness not to press for every clause it desired; and (3) the limited usefulness of the injunction and the yellow-dog contract to most employers, and their seeming unfairness. Like the La Follette Act of 1915, the Norris-LaGuardia Act represented limited legislation which was capable of enlisting support from more than just those who were concerned with the interests of organized labor.

The coming of the New Deal and the subsequent passage of the Wagner Act is often viewed as a major turning point in public policy. The explanations range from the triumph of civil over property rights through the failure of the business mythology, to the access of labor to political power. There are two problems in these explanations. One is, that despite the profound impact of the Wagner Act, its passage marked no great break with the past. The other is that they provide no basis upon which to explain the seeming reversals contained in the Taft-Hartley and Landrum-Griffin Acts. The Wagner Act, it should be recalled, follows the National Industrial Recovery Act and Public Resolution 44. The former was primarily a business bill with Section 7A tossed in because one-fourth of the labor force was unemployed. Public Resolution 44 hardly represented a victory for organized labor since it did not correct the major problem, the lack of enforcement power. The Wagner Act was then essentially an accident. Its chief sponsor believed in organized labor as a solution to the economic problem of the period. In addition, business had given short shrift to the mildly expressed policy of the employees' right to organize. The election of 1934 made the legislature responsive to major change. And perhaps most important, the agriculturists were willing to approve the Act so long as farm labor was excluded.

Thus a bill passed which could not pass the year before and probably not a year later.

The Taft-Hartley and the Landrum-Griffin Acts fit neatly into the same pattern. The growth of unions during the 1930s and 1940s resulted in their position receiving a more sympathetic view in Congress. This was sufficient to prevent the passage of unfavorable bills for a number of years. Why then did it fail to prevent the passage of the Taft-Hartley and Landrum-Griffin Acts? Part of the explanation lies in poor tactics. In the face of external circumstances which built up pressure for some legislation, the post-World War II wave of strikes for Taft-Hartley, and the McClellan Committee's parade of union misconduct for Landrum-Griffin, organized labor was sharply divided and unwilling to accept minimal changes. This tended to alienate many legislators and to weaken the position of supporters of labor. More important, external circumstances made the interests of organized labor appear to be opposed to those of the general public, a reversal of their image in 1935.

What then, for the future? The decline of employment in those occupations which have been the heart of the union movement, coupled with an apparent inability to organize in expanding occupations necessarily means a continuing decline in labor's congressional power. Thus one can predict with reasonable confidence that, if in the future, activities associated with organized labor affect or can be made to appear to affect adversely large groups of lay members or outsiders, additional "anti-labor" legislation will result. The only favorable legislation which can be expected will deal with employees as distinct from organized employees, such as Social Security or Area Redevelopment, or will be limited legislation previously agreed to by all of the segments of organized labor and management which will be affected.

To many observers this latter type of legislation, that which represents the consensus of the involved parties, is the ideal. They view our historical pattern as too dependent upon isolated pressures, as, for example, the depression, and the post-World War II wave of strikes. While this view has merit, it is difficult to conceive of the required resolution of interests except on an industry-by-industry basis and resulting in a number of formal labor policies. Such a solution probably would not appeal to Congress or to the public. Perhaps more germane is the observation that if the parties can reach such a consensus, they are free to follow it rather than to be guided by formal policy.

SUGGESTED READINGS

EDWARD BERMAN, *Labor and the Sherman Act*, New York: Harper & Row, 1930.

IRVING BERNSTEIN, *The Lean Years*, Boston: Houghton-Mifflin, 1960, Chap. 11.

IRVING BERNSTEIN, *The New Deal Collective Bargaining Policy*, Berkeley: University of California Press, 1950.

ARCHIBALD COX, *Law and National Labor Policy*, Institute of Industrial Relations Monograph Series No. 5, Los Angeles: University of California Press, 1960.

FELIX FRANKFURTER AND NATHAN GREENE, *The Labor Injunction*, New York: Macmillan, 1930.

GERALD POMPER, "Labor and Congress: The Repeal of Taft-Hartley," *Labor History II*, Fall, 1961, pp. 323–343.

ARTHUR M. SCHLESINGER, JR., *The Coming of the New Deal*, Boston: Houghton-Mifflin, 1958.

JOHN S. SMITH, "Organized Labor and Government in the Wilson Era; 1913–1921: Some Conclusions," *Labor History III*, Fall, 1962.

HYMAN WEINTRAUB, *Andrew Furuseth, Emancipator of the Seamen*, Berkeley: University of California Press, 1959

CHAPTER 5

The Proper Study
of Public Policy

The preamble to our basic labor law states that the inability of workers to bargain with their employers leads to imbalance in the distribution of income and to a lack of economic stability. The text of the law discusses the rights which are guaranteed to workers and the activities which are forbidden to unions and to firms. The spread of collective bargaining under the Act was accomplished by the growth of large national unions. This in turn has led to multiemployer bargaining units, pattern bargaining, etc., which have shaped the content of the collective agreements. Part of the negotiated content has undoubtedly influenced congressional action, such as the relationship between the growth of private pensions and the granting of increased benefits under Social Security. Where then does one draw the boundaries in a study of the impact of federal labor policy?

Situations which have been directly influenced by, and are closely tied to, the on-going decisions rendered under the Acts would appear to be the appropriate ones to study. A good case can be made for the proposition that the passage of the Wagner

Act was the key to the large growth of independent national unionism in this country. Yet, the growth and development of unions have been influenced by numerous other factors and forces and it would be preferable to make these the object of a separate study. In like manner, the pattern of incomes, wages, productivity, and profits in today's economy has been determined in only a small degree by the Wagner and Taft-Hartley laws. This leaves us two areas, both closely tied to the development of policy under the labor statutes. The first is the development and rationale for the decisions which have been made. The second is the extent to which these decisions have meant that workers have actually enjoyed the rights which are theirs under the Act. Additionally, where some of the decisions appear to have direct economic consequences, some attention will be given to the direction and magnitude of the consequences.

In the chapters which consider the substantive problems, much of the emphasis is necessarily upon the patterns in the narrow set of cases attached to each area. The patterns in the different areas may be more meaningful if some consideration is first given to alternative ways of examining the behavior of courts and the extent to which the NLRB's approach to a particular problem may reflect policy considerations which relate to the whole of labor law, and not merely to the aspect in question.

COURTS AND POLICY

There are several approaches to a consideration of the behavior of the courts. The first, a standard and widely used method, is one which seeks to trace the evolution and meaning of particular policies by an analysis of the various administrative agency and court decisions. It is derived from the procedure used by lawyers in preparing their briefs. The desired results are: (1) an understanding of the process by which the current position of the agency or court was obtained; and (2) an insight into the aspects of those decisions which logically imply partial conflict with a line of decisions in a different area of policy. A principal weakness in this system stems from its failure to view the generation of legal decisions in its wider contexts. Specifically, the system may fail to illumine the crucial elements which have contributed to molding a particular line of decisions. In addition, it fails to recognize that goals or reactions of the various Board members or justices may not coincide. Consequently, a change in the composition of the decision makers may alter the trend of decisions.

The second method would be to devise a system that concentrated on the key elements in each case. Such a system would involve the selection of a particular series of cases, identification of their common elements, and an attempt to produce an empirical weighting system which would allow the Court's position on future cases to be predicted.

To date, studies following this pattern have met with little real success. It is not difficult to understand why. If the system is to consider very many variables, it requires a large sample of cases. For most aspects of policy this means that cases decided over a span of a number of years must be used. When these cases are used the engine of analysis assumes that the world has not changed between the time when the first case was decided until the date of the last decision. Yet, over the years, a number of changes do take place. The easiest one to observe is the changing membership of the Court. For example, of the nine members of the United States Supreme Court when its 1952 term opened, only three remained ten years later. In addition, the Court may make a dramatic change in its view as it did in 1936–1937.

In *Carter* v. *Carter Coal Co.*[1] (1936) the Supreme Court held that the Guffey Coal Act was unconstitutional on the grounds that its use of the NIRA code idea to fix prices and its allowance of collective bargaining involved excessive stretching of the commerce power. Then in *NLRB* v. *Jones & Laughlin Steel Corp.*[2]

[1] *Carter* v. *Carter Coal Co.*, 298 U.S. 238 (1936).
[2] *NLRB* v. *Jones and Laughlin Steel Corp.*, 301 U.S. 1 (1937); 1 LRRM 703.

(1937) it held that the Wagner Act which established collective
bargaining over a much broader range of industries was constitutional.

The process may also be evolutionary. One study in this area
tried to predict the Supreme Court's behavior in cases involving
state court decisions concerning a defendant's right to counsel.
The relative importance of such reasonable factors as seriousness
of the crime and age of the defendant gradually evolved to
include a number of other factors until at last in *Gideon* v. *Wainwright*[3] (1963) the Court held the right to counsel to be absolute.
In *Escobedo* v. *Illinois*[4] (1964) the rule was extended to include the period between the time a person becomes a prime
suspect until his trial.

An additional weakness for a study of the Supreme Court
stems from the fact that it has the authority to choose the cases
which it will hear. It does this by its grant of certiorari and by its
refusal to hear an appeal, because of a lack of a substantial federal
question. Consequently, an examination of only those cases which
are heard by the Supreme Court may fail to indicate the very
important weight of factor X, the absence of which may preclude
a case from even being considered by the Court. Lastly, the absence of any theory upon which the judges' actions are said to be
based means that there is no basis for estimating the tradeoff
between important and less important factors in the minds of the
judges. For example, if severity of the crime and age of the defendant are both important, how many years of age are necessary
to make up for an extra five years of maximum sentence?

The third system of analysis is to set up a matrix consisting of
the individual judges or agency members and the cases decided
each year and record in it each individual's vote in every case.
This can be used to calculate the extent to which each member
votes with, or in opposition to, every other member. Such a procedure is useful in several respects: (1) it will indicate the type

---

[3] *Gideon* v. *Wainwright*, 372 U.S. 335 (1963).
[4] *Escobedo* v. *Illinois*, 378 U.S. 478 (1964); 32 LW 4605.

of cases and issues which divide the court or agency; (2) it will show whether the voting blocs are stable over a broad range of issues or whether the composition of the blocs varies depending upon the type of case considered; and (3) it allows the impact upon existing blocs of a change in membership to be examined. The usefulness of the bloc system for predicting the future course of the court or agency is less clear. Voting bloc membership is partly a function of the personality and intellectual influence of its chief member, so an examination of that member's views as indicated in speeches, publications, etc., may give some insight into the future course of the bloc. Additionally, if some members do not appear to belong to particular blocs but are usually found voting with the majority on cases which divide the court, the views of these pivotal members may provide a clue to future decisions on issues which sharply divide the court or agency.

One area where an analysis of voting bloc behavior has been helpful is in the behavior of the Supreme Court in handling cases arising under the Federal Employers Liability Act. Railroad workers injured in the course of their employment do not, as do most employees, receive workmen's compensation. Rather, they must sue their employer on the grounds of negligence. Why Congress and the railroad unions have resisted changing this lottery into true workmen's compensation is an interesting question but one without a simple answer. Given that the major point at issue in most of these cases will involve matters of fact, and considering that the Court accepts only about 10 percent of all cases coming to it on certiorari, a natural first expectation would be that very few FELA cases would be considered. This expectation would be realized were one to consider that of 71 petitions filed by railroads between 1938 and 1954 in cases where sufficiency of evidence was the principal question, only 1 was granted, and it was later dismissed as improvidently granted. Cases appealed by workers appear to be different, for here 36 of 78 similar petitions were granted.

One explanation for the divergence in the treatment of two

classes of petitioners would be that at least four justices (the number needed to grant certiorari) believed that: (1) the requirement of a suit was unfair to the workers; and (2) in the absence of congressional action every effort should be made to assist the employee to recover damages. A recent case may illustrate the equity of their position.[5] An employee worked in a station which was operated by one railroad but which serviced another railroad as well. A defective car door on a train of the railroad for whom he did not work injured him. Had he been employed by the railroad with the defective car, there is no question but that he could have recovered damages. Similarly, were railroads under a workmen's compensation statute, this employee would have been compensated. Yet, in this instance, it required the intervention of the Supreme Court to assure him damages.

The fact that the Supreme Court appears to give special consideration to railroad workers' cases raises several questions. Why don't they take all the workers' cases instead of only about one-half? There are two possible answers. One is, that if only four justices feel strongly about workers' cases, they can only grant certiorari. In order to insure that the worker wins his case, the four who vote for certiorari must select cases where they can obtain the vote of at least one other justice when the merits of the case are considered. A second is, even if five justices wished to assist workers, it would be difficult to publicly justify their acceptance of all worker petitions. This suggests that the proper strategy would be to accept cases in which the worker had won in the district court and lost in the appeals court. All others would be rejected with the exception of a few in which the worker had lost in both lower courts, but where the evidence was such that it would not be unreasonable to believe that a different lower court might have handled it in another way.

An examination of recent Supreme Court treatment of Federal Employers Liability Act cases will show that what has happened is exactly what was expected, thus giving strong support

[5] *Shenker* v. *Baltimore & Ohio Railroad*, 374 U.S. 1 (1963).

for the belief that special treatment has been granted to this class of case. The extent of this special treatment can be seen in the following rather extreme example.

Prior to reporting for work at 4:45 P.M. on October 7, 1950, Boyd R. Ringhiser took a laxative because of constipation problems. When he arrived at his place of employment, he used the bathroom at the roundhouse. He then boarded his engine and picked up a string of cars. While waiting for an air brake test, he had an urgent call of nature. He left the locomotive to go to a rest room across a few tracks. Before he could reach it, a string of empties passed between him and his goal. Not being able to wait until it had passed, he went to another track and climbed into a low-sided gondola car. While thus engaged, another train crew switched two cars onto that track, and one of them bumped the car next to his which came in contact with his car. The bump was normal for a switching operation but the contact caused the load of steel plates in the gondala to shift crushing Ringhiser's leg so that in a few days it had to be amputated.[6]

Was the employer negligent under the law in this case? Yes (5–4), said the Supreme Court. This case forms an interesting contrast with a decision many years before by the same Massachusetts Judge Shaw who handed down *Commonwealth* v. *Hunt*. In this second case he held the railroad not to be negligent and responsible for injuries to a Boston train crew occasioned by the error of a Worcester switchman. The grounds were that the fellow servant rule applied and an employee should be aware of, and guard against the weaknesses of his fellow employee.[7] The apparent pattern in the Supreme Court's treatment of railroad workers who have been injured in the cause of their employment is suggestive that an examination of the NLRB may yield similar informative patterns.

---

[6] *Ringhiser* v. *Chesapeake and Ohio Railroad Co.*, 354 U.S. 901 (1957).
[7] *Farwell* v. *Boston and Worcester Railroad Co.*, 4 Metcalf 49 (Mass. 1842).

THE NLRB AND ITS POLICIES

The "New Frontier" NLRB has been charged with being pro-labor. Its predecessor was alleged to have been pro-business as in the following quotation.

The quest of the new Board [the Eisenhower one in 1953] for policy changes, and for replacement of employees in policy positions, raised questions as to the independent, impartial, nonpolitical, and quasi-judicial status of the new Board.[8]

The attacks are generally supported by reference to a few well-publicized cases or those where the precedents of the old Board have been overruled. One problem is that the most recent reversal may only represent a return to an earlier doctrine. The following series of cases is a good illustration of what can happen. Consider a situation where a firm and a union have a history of collective bargaining for a particular unit of employees. If, some years after such a unit has come into being, another union wishes to represent the old unit plus certain additional employees, or the present union wishes to enlarge the unit to include these previously un-represented workers, how is this handled?

It has been handled in two different ways. In *Petersen and Lytle*,[9] decided in 1945, the Board held that the formerly excluded employees could vote upon whether they wished to be included in the same unit with the other employees. If they voted not to be included, the matter was dropped if there wasn't a second union. If there was a second union, an election was held in the old unit to see which union would be the representative. The rationale for this procedure was that it allowed the minority employees a real opportunity to control their situation. Their wishes would then not be swallowed up by those of the larger

[8] From Pucinski, p. 529.
[9] *Petersen and Lytle*, 60 NLRB 1070 (1945); 16 LRRM 27.

group. Then in 1950 in *Waterous*,[10] with two members of the Board dissenting, this policy was overturned. The NLRB decided that if the newly requested (combined) unit was an appropriate one, a single election would be held for that unit and the newly added employees would have no prior vote concerning their wishes. Four years passed and another reversal of policy occurred. In *Zia*,[11] a three-man majority with one member dissenting held that if the previously unrepresented workers wished to be considered part of the larger unit, they would be, and if they didn't, then they wouldn't be. This overturned *Waterous* and was a return to the views given in *Petersen and Lytle*. More years passed, there were more new members, and again the policy was changed, this time by a 3–2 vote. In *D.V. Displays*[12] the Zia policy was overturned and a return was made to the concept of a single election in the newly enlarged unit containing the old represented group and the newly added ones. This constituted a return to the *Waterous* (1950) policy.

In addition to being very general in their nature, the charges of bias against the Board are suspect because they are usually made by individuals who disagree with the trend of decisions or who see certain ones as adverse to their own interests. In reply to the charges and in defense of their decisions, Board members will often emphasize the large number of cases in which there has been agreement among both old and new Board members, and the equally large number of cases where the decisions have been favorable to the interests of the group whom the attacking individual represents. They also stress that they must administer the Act as they read it. In the words of a former chairman of the NLRB, Guy Farmer:

My job is to interpret the law as I read it, not as somebody else who preceded me thought it should be read. I would not be so foolhardy as

[10] *Waterous Co.*, 92 NLRB 76 (1950); 27 LRRM 1050.
[11] *Zia Co.*, 108 NLRB 1134 (1954); 34 LRRM 1133.
[12] *D.V. Displays Corp.*, 134 NLRB 568 (1961); 49 LRRM 1199.

to blandly disregard the opinions of my predecessors, but I took an oath to administer the statute, not someone else's view as to what the statute means. I would not have taken the job, and I certainly would not remain in it if I thought that my sole function was to administer the statute in a straight-jacket fashioned by the interpretations made by my predecessors on the Board. The precedents which we have over-ruled were the opinions of the prior Board as to what the statute meant and how it applied to particular situations. Since we did not agree with their interpretations, we have no choice but to reverse them. If the charge that we are legislating were made in good faith, we would plead not guilty. But if it be true that we have legislated, we have done nothing more than repeal an improper legislative act of the prior Board.[13]

Even granting that the Board members render nothing less than an honest effort to interpret the statute as they understand it and as they believe Congress intended it to be read, it is still useful to examine the type of behavior which would characterize a Board that wished to favor a particular group. Since the Board is thought to be quasi-judicial in character, a freely acknowledged, semipolitical approach to decisions would be a source of trouble. Similarly, an unacknowledged political approach which was readily apparent would also be undesirable. These considerations lead to the expectation that the approaches utilized would be generalized, designed to be favorable on balance to the group whose interests the appointees' political party favored, but not necessarily to be favorable in every instance. Given the NLRB's heavy case load, a broad-gauged approach would be easier to incorporate. One system which meets these requirements is what can be termed the "per se" approach. It states that if the actions in a particular case are used as a weapon against the side to be favored, they should be ruled automatically illegal regardless of the attending circumstances. If the actions assist the side to be favored, they should be viewed on a case-by-case basis which would stress the impacts of the actions and which would demand clear proof of coercion and

[13] From a speech by Gerald A. Brown, "Labor Laws in Equilibrium," reported in *Daily Labor Report*, September 30, 1963, pp. D–3.

not just a few isolated examples. Illustrative of this "per se" approach are the following.

One of the Eisenhower Board critics, David McDonald, president of the Steelworkers, said:

Under the old Board, there was a long standing doctrine that it was an unfair labor practice for an employer to question his employees about union membership and activities. Yet, fundamental as this doctrine was, it was overturned by the new Board in *Blue Flash Express, Inc.*[14]

The particular rule in question dates from *Standard Coosa Thatcher*.[15] In that case a Truman Board decided that any interrogation of an employee concerning his or other's union activities was an unfair labor practice. In *Blue Flash*[16] the determination was merely that the "test is whether under all circumstances the exercise of rights is restrained or interfered with." This was hardly an earth-shaking conclusion. In fact, as early as *Sax* v. *NLRB*[17] in 1948, the Second Circuit Court had held that "such perfunctory, innocuous remarks and queries standing alone are insufficient to support a finding of a violation of the Act." And prior to *Blue Flash* there were 11 other circuit court decisions where *Thatcher*-type decisions were overturned. Thus, rather than being politically motivated as the critic suggested, the Board could have defended itself by saying that it was merely bowing to the superior wit and judgment of the reviewing courts.

Why, if the courts had taken such a dim view of the whole process, should the Board have continued its practice? In part this is because the Board, while recognizing the judgments of the Supreme Court, has never been willing to be dictated to by the circuit courts on matters where they and the Board differ. An alternative explanation is also apparent if the Board's behavior is seen as an attempt to support either unions or managements. Be-

[14] From Pucinski, p. 530.
[15] *Standard Coosa Thatcher*, 85 NLRB 1358 (1949); 24 LRRM 1575.
[16] *Blue Flash Express Inc.*, 109 NLRB 591 (1954), 34 LRRM 1384.
[17] *Sax* v. *NLRB*, 171 F 769 (1948); 23 LRRM 2191.

tween *Thatcher* and *Blue Flash* the NLRB decided 144 cases of interrogation, 30 of which went to the circuit courts, and 12 of which were overturned. These 144, on an average basis, would represent some 2880 charges of interrogation brought before the regional offices. How many of these charges involved *Thatcher*-type charges is unknown, but if it is assumed that the ratio of reversed interrogation cases to all interrogation cases in the circuit courts represents the ratio of *Thatcher*-type charges to all interrogation charges, about 1150 *Thatcher*-type charges were made, some of which were handled by the employer according to the inflexible Board rule. In addition, a number of other employees may have refrained from acting. Thus the policy here might be characterized by saying that an employer could ask no questions concerning union activity unless he were prepared to go to a circuit court in which case he could ask those which did not of themselves coerce his employees in the exercise of their rights.

Cases involving picketing are also susceptible to this approach. One section of the Landrum-Griffin amendment to the Taft-Hartley law states:

> That nothing in this subparagraph shall be construed to prohibit any picketing or other publicity for the purpose of truthfully advising the public (including consumers) that an employer does not employ members of, or have a contract with, a labor organization, unless an effect of such picketing is to induce any individual employed by any other person in the course of his employment not to pick up, deliver, or transport any goods or not to perform any services.

The section quoted above is clear enough—or is it? How many deliveries and over what period would have to be prevented in order to have the picketing prohibited? Those who wished to favor unions would be apt to insist that there be a number of stoppages and that adequate substitutes were not available to the employer. One of contrary view might find a single refusal to transport sufficient to invoke the statute.

In *Barker Brothers*[18] the union had posted publicity pickets. In the course of the picketing at least five and perhaps more stoppages and delays of delivery took place because of the existence of the pickets. In each instance the delay was only temporary.

The Board did not find a violation. It concluded that the stoppages had to "interfere with, disrupt or curtail the employer's business" in order for there to be a violation of the law. Two members of the Board dissented, arguing that even a single stoppage was cause to invoke the Act.

This type of Board determination, of not looking at whether the employee or employer has been coerced, but only at the action of the company or the union, appears to have been utilized by all Boards. It has usually been viewed in less than a favorable light by the reviewing courts. This judicial lack of respect for "per se" need not have been. It is true that the Act provides that an individual has to have been coerced and that the finding of "per se" violations or allowable acts does not allow for the test of whether the action has coerced the particular individual. This can be seen vividly by considering how the same action by an employer would have a markedly different impact upon a Detroit truck driver and a weaver in a southern textile mill. Still, the reviewing courts could easily have held that since the NLRB is an expert body it was within its rights in determining that *any* action of a particular type did or did not result in coercion. Such an allowance would at least have had the positive virtue of making it very clear exactly what could and could not be done under the Act. On the other hand, given a changing national political climate, the unwillingness of the Courts to accept a "per se" approach has made the transition between Boards easier because new policies can be developed by stressing factual differences in cases rather than by directly overturning prior precedents.

Many of the activities under the Act revolve around the deter-

---

[18] *Barker Brothers Corp.* v. *Gold's Inc.*, 138 NLRB 478 (1962); 51 LRRM 1053; affirmed 328 F. 2d 431; 55 LRRM 2544.

mination of the desires of employees toward formal organization. Board determinations in these areas may also exhibit some particular patterns. During a campaign for union representation, an employer may choose to actively oppose the union. His activities may include communications to the workers in an attempt to influence their votes, or they may affect only a few employees. In addition, some or all of the employer's moves may be legal or illegal, fair or unfair.

To deal with actions by the employer, or the union, the Board has several alternatives. If workers have been unjustly discharged, they can be reinstated and paid their lost earnings plus 6 percent. Where communications have coerced the employees, the offending party can be ordered to stop and to post a notice indicating future compliance with the law. In both these instances the party which lost the election can obtain a rerun of the election. It may be that the actions complained of were not illegal but were in some sense unfair, in which case the election can also be ordered to be rerun. The following examples indicate the different patterns of Board behavior which may be observed.

As we shall see when the subject is treated at greater length in Chapter 8, the limits of employer speech are difficult to determine. Because of this, different Boards have been able to move in diverse directions. One company sent a letter to its employees which pointed out that the union which desired to represent them had other contracts in the area whose provisions were inferior to the workers' current conditions. It went on to state that the company had excellent fringe benefits and that these would be improved over the years, union or not. What, the firm asked, could the union offer but trouble in the possibility of strikes, lost income, and required monthly dues payments? In saying this, was the company only engaging in a prediction of what would happen, or was the statement a veiled threat? A reasonable man could read it either way and a Board which favored one side could decide the case with equal ease.

The employer may have taken direct action and discharged a

few workers who were known to be active union members. The employer's defense may be that the discharge was for reasons other than the employee's union activity. It will then be necessary to determine if the employer's alternative explanation can be rejected and illegal discrimination inferred. This is often difficult if there is no other evidence to give credence to an anti-union image of the company. The expectation would be that a Board favorable to unions would tend to take a dim view of the dismissal of very active unionists, regardless of the cause cited by the company. Conversely, a Board which favored the employer would tend to give the benefit of the doubt, if at all reasonable, to the company's explanation. How, for example, should this be handled?

In the *Tex-O-Kan*[19] case the secretary of the union and a co-worker were fired by a company guilty of other unfair labor practices, including the discharge of the previous union secretary. The reason given for their discharge was that they had put 280 bags of flour into the wrong sacks, which they had. Another employee testified that two days later the manager said the reason for firing the secretary was a pretext and that he was going to fire the whole "damned bunch." This testimony of the employee was denied by the manager. The Board decided that the discharge was because of union activity. The Fifth Circuit Court overruled on the grounds that the employer had an adequate reason for discharge regardless of union activities.

Finally, generally those actions occurring just before the vote which appear to be unfair can be the basis for ordering a new election. Since unfairness is difficult to define, there is ample room for members to lean one way or another. An election was held in St. Louis one very cold day. The man from the NLRB office could not get his car started, nor could he get a taxi. He finally obtained a ride from the company's personnel director. If the union loses, should the election be overturned because some of the employees might have believed the NLRB to favor management? Perhaps the NLRB should be as Caesar's wife, but what happens if the

[19] *NLRB* v. *Tex-O-Kan*, 122 F. 2d 433 (1941); 8 LRRM 675.

NLRB representative arrives in a union (nonunion) taxi? The possibility for a Board whose sympathy lies one way or the other is clear. The present Board upheld the Regional Office decision to hold a new election.

It may no longer be true that "No Contract, No Work" is an inviolate union rule. But it certainly is true that "No Union, No Collective Bargaining" is. Consequently, the cause of unionism or the easy life of the employer will best be served by decisions which aid or impede the ability of unions to win representation elections. The defensive moves by the employer have already been discussed. Even more basic may be the determination of the appropriate unit. Under the Wagner Act, units that were very small and whose chief claim to fame was the high probability that the union would win the election were sometimes certified as appropriate by the Board. In the *May Company*[20] case, a unit of 28 busheling employees was determined as an appropriate unit even though there were 5000 store employees, and in *Carolina Coach*[21] the division was by states, because employees in one state favored unions and those in the other did not. Congress, when it rewrote the Act in 1947, viewed cases like the above with less than favor and a clause was inserted stating that in unit determinations the extent of union organization was not to be the controlling factor. This is not as restrictive as it might seem, since except in special circumstances, it is not clear that any specific unit is more appropriate than any other. Consequently, a Board is generally able to justify any unit it favors.

If hand-tailored units depending upon union sentiment favor unions, it seems reasonable that the larger the number and more dispersed the employees in the unit, the more difficult will be organization. Consequently, units like these will favor management. How might large bargaining units be obtained? Perhaps the use of employer policy as the criterion for proper unit determina-

[20] *May Department Stores* v. *NLRB*, 326 U.S. 376 (1945); 17 LRRM 643.
[21] *Carolina Scenic Coach Lines*, 33 NLRB 528 (1941); 8 LRRM 281.

tion is the answer. What is more natural, if Mr. Smith handles employment policy for plants A, B, and C, than to rule that the three plants should have a common bargaining unit? A single illustration will suffice. In *Father and Son Shoe Stores*[22] the union requested a single unit composed of the 37 stores in the Chicago area, but would accept each store as a unit. The company desired the 48 stores in its Chicago district composed of 32 in Chicago, 5 in the suburbs, 10 within 15–90 miles of Chicago, and 1 between 180–190 miles of the city. The 48-store unit was approved.

The current Board swung in an opposite direction in *Sav-On-Drugs*.[23] The employer wished to have the nine stores in his administrative area declared as the appropriate unit, or failing this, since the nine were located in both New York and New Jersey, he would have been content to have had only the New Jersey stores constitute the unit. The Board, however, agreed with the union that the single store which it had requested was an appropriate unit.

Yet, even before an election can be held, a unit chosen, or an unfair labor practice filed, the employer must be subject to the Act. Thus, within certain limits, a board can draw in or exclude certain employees. Since the scope of the Act embraces the broadest reach of the commerce clause, the Board's self-limitations on extensions might seem unimportant. It should be recalled that: (1) only 30 percent of the states have comprehensive labor relations statutes; and (2) many of the employees utilizing the services of the Board are in small bargaining units. Twenty-five percent of the elections concern units of less than ten employees. Most states have less effectual or less liberal policies. Thus, it can be seen that the assertion of jurisdiction by the NLRB can be interpreted as an action favorable to the union position. A few cases will illustrate some of the considerations involved.

A service station lessee fired several of his employees, seemingly for union activities. The Board held the lessee to really be an

---

[22] *Father and Son Shoe Stores*, 117 NLRB 1497 (1951); 40 LRRM 1032.
[23] *Sav-On-Drugs*, 138 NLRB 1032 (1962); 51 LRRM 1152.

employee of the oil company which owned the station. It found
the company guilty of the unfair labor practice committed by its
agent. The nub of the case turned on the independent contractor-
employee status of the lessee. While the Board and courts insist
that no one factor is determining in cases like these, the current
NLRB places great weight upon who determines the final price
of the good or service and the extent to which an individual must
handle only a single firm's products, restricted to a particular
geographical area. In another instance, the unlicensed seamen on
the ships of the Woods Hole Oceanographic Institute wished to
hold an election to select a representative. While the Institute
is big enough to meet the normal Board standards as a nonprofit
institution, it would normally have been held to be outside the
jurisdiction of the Board. The Board, pointing to the Institute's
work in sonar, took jurisdiction. The justification was the substantial impact upon national defense exerted by the Institute.

INDIVIDUALS, GROUPS, AND POLICY

In addition to the role of public or official actions, private actions also influence policy. An example of this type of procedure
occurred in Illinois a few years ago. The Metropolitan Fair and
Exposition Authority[24] which was to build an exhibition hall at
23rd Street and the Lake in Chicago was unable to sell its bonds.
It seemed as if its many opponents had finally won. Then the State
Treasurer announced that the State would purchase the bonds.
The opponents went to court to try to prevent the Treasurer from
purchasing the bonds. There was almost no chance that the final
decision of the courts would deny the Treasurer the right to buy
the bonds. The matter was one of judgment, of whether the
Authority was a reasonable and prudent investment for state
funds. In matters like this, judges are wont to give the benefit of

[24] The story of the Metropolitan Fair and Exposition is more fully reported in Edward C. Banfield, *Political Influence*, Glencoe: The Free Press,
1961, ch. 7.

any doubts to the elected officials. The value of the suit to the opponents was not in judgment, but in delay. A case like this might be dragged out two or three years, especially if some way could be found to get the case to the United States Supreme Court. Faced with a situation like this the Authority might be willing to compromise, or even better, the probability of a new Treasurer, unwilling to buy the bonds, being elected in the fall of 1958 was very high. Suit was filed late in January of 1958 with a request for a trial date in May. The judge set the trial for March 17. Then another lawyer asked and was granted permission to intervene. He did this in order to raise issues not in the original suit. Had this not been done, these other issues could have been raised after final judgment, thus adding more years of delay. On May 1 the judge decided against the plaintiffs. Appeal to the State Supreme Court would have been delayed until the last possible day had not the intervening plaintiff appealed the day the decision was handed down. On August 1, acting during their normal vacation period, the Supreme Court held for the defendants.

Within the area of labor policy, private influence will typically consist of:

1. Violations of the law knowingly undertaken in the hope that: (a) no one will complain; (b) faced with the guilty party's determination to carry out a protracted legal battle, no one will complain; and (c) the remedies of the NLRB will not defeat the intent of the violator.
2. The use of delay to impose one's illegal will.
3. Employing one's superior financial position to make the assertion of the other person's rights too costly.

The success of some of these actions can be seen in the following.

1. A union obtained 100 signed cards in a firm of approximately 120 employees. The company opposed the union, and before the election, discharged several union supporters. Since the NLRB

does not hold elections where unfair labor practice charges are outstanding, the union was faced with the alternative of letting the election go ahead and then filing unfair labor practice charges for the discharged workers or filing the charges and delaying the election up to two years. The union took its chance with the election and lost 50 to 30. The company then agreed to pay back wages to the discharged employees without formal board hearings.

2. A union engaged in a secondary boycott. The company affected appealed to the closest Regional Director of the NLRB. He then investigated to see whether there was a secondary boycott. If he found one, he was required by law to seek an injunction against the boycott. When the Regional Director investigated, however, he found that it had been voluntarily ended. The few days of its existence had been sufficient and the employer had come to terms.

3. The use of delay for less than legal purposes is clearly underlined in this quotation from the Associate Counsel of the Textile Workers Union:

Also when the company gets up and says you were fired and will never work here again, the workers notice 3–1 their case will be won if it is fought. I do not know what kind of heroes you've got in this world but you are asking a lot of married men with children to take a 3–1 chance to be fired twice, and maybe get your job back after waiting two years.[25]

4. The use of superior wealth to defeat the purposes of the National Labor Relations Act is not as important as in other areas of labor relations where the plaintiff has to pay his own legal fees and may not be able to obtain judgment for them. The old adage about only poor murderers being executed is not without meaning here. The principal difficulty under the NLRA is that back pay, even with the newly added 6 percent interest, is not sufficient, for the worker needs current income and probably cannot borrow

[25] From Pucinski, p. 239.

funds at 6 percent. What is needed is reinstatement upon the issuance of a complaint.

The chapters which follow deal with specific substantive issues. To accomplish this, consideration must be given to the development of specific concepts of allowable and unallowable conduct. Yet in this, the whole of policy is not merely the sum of the particular areas. The true impact of certain sections, like the duty to bargain, may be less of a function of what the duty requires than it is of the jurisdictional broadness of its application.

In this chapter I have tried to indicate some of the characteristics of policy determination which should be remembered as one studies specific issues. In a sense, what has been said is that administrative agencies and courts are multidimensional in impact and character. Consequently, while consideration of the isolated cases attached to one issue alone will give insights into the trees, it is necessary to take a wider view of labor policy in order to properly illuminate the forest and its pathways.

SUGGESTED READINGS

FRANKLIN M. FISHER, "The Mathematical Analysis of Supreme Court Decisions: The Use and Abuse of Quantitative Methods," *The American Political Science Review*, LII, June, 1958, pp. 321–338.

HENRY J. FRIENDLY, *The Federal Administrative Agencies*, Cambridge: Harvard University Press, 1962.

GLENDON A. SCHUBERT, *The Quantitative Analysis of Judicial Behavior*, Glencoe, Ill.: The Free Press, 1959.

CHAPTER 6

The Duty to Bargain

HISTORICAL DEVELOPMENT

For practical purposes, the federal government's promotion of collective bargaining began during World War I when some agencies included in the contracts which they granted a guarantee of the right of the contractor's employees to engage in collective bargaining. Subsequently, the War Labor Conference Board recommended that, in addition to the right of recognition, employee organizations be given the right to bargain collectively. These recommendations were incorporated with the establishment of the War Labor Board, in President Wilson's proclamation of April 1918. Practices under the Board did not make clear the duties which had been placed upon the employers by the bargaining requirement. This probably stemmed in part from the fact that the Board's status was not derived from legislation. Of greater importance was the fact that the Board, rather than sending disputes over substantive issues back to the parties for bargaining, would decide the issues as it saw their merits.

The definition of the content of the duty to bargain became no clearer when it was applied to the various arrangements concerning the railroad industry between World War I and the great depres-

sion. Thus, when Section 7a of the National Industrial Recovery
Act provided that employees would have the right to "bargain
collectively," it was left to the National Labor Board to give meaning to the words. The Board held:

> True collective bargaining involves more than the holding of confer-
> ences and the exchange of pleasantries. It is not limited to the settle-
> ment of specific grievances. . . . While the law does not compel the
> parties to reach agreement, it does contemplate that both parties will
> approach the negotiations with an open mind and will make a reason-
> able effort to reach a common ground of agreement.[1]

In line with this, it was decided that pre-emptory rejection of
employee proposals or a refusal to reduce an agreement to written
form were forbidden. It seems likely that this Board would have
gone on to require companies to offer some "reasonable" counterproposals. Before such a case arose, the NRA Board was replaced
and it was left to its successor, the (old) NLRB in the famous
Houde Engineering Corporation [2] case, to put forward the position
that, to bargain in good faith, an employer must match proposals
with counterproposals and in addition make every reasonable effort
to reach agreement. During its brief existence, however, this Board
did not go on to judge the soundness of any employer proposals.

It is within this briefly sketched context that the Wagner Act
was introduced, discussed, and passed. Nothing within that process, however, dealt with an elaboration of what had already been
implied concerning the requirements of the duty to bargain. At
several points Senator Wagner referred with approval to the reasoning in the *Houde* case, but he did not amplify on its meaning.
The report of the Senate Committee added little, saying:

> . . . It seems clear that a guarantee of the right of employees to
> bargain collectively through representatives of their own choosing is a
> mere delusion if it is not accompanied by the correlative duty on the
> part of the other party to recognize such representatives as they have

[1] *Connecticut Coke Co.*, 2 NLB 88 (1934) at 89.
[2] *Houde Engineering Corporation*, 1 NLRB (old) 35 (1934).

been designated (whether as individuals or labor organizations) and to negotiate with them in a bona fide effort to arrive at a collective bargaining agreement. Furthermore, the procedure of holding governmentally supervised elections to determine the choice of representatives of employees becomes of little worth if after the election its results are for all practical purposes ignored.[3]

Other comments on this requirement were essentially answers by Senators Wagner and Walsh (Chairman of the Committee on Education and Labor) to fear expressed by some employers that they were going to be forced to agree to certain specific but unidentified provisions. It was within this quite limited context that Walsh gave his often quoted:

. . . The Bill indicates the method and manner in which employees may organize, the method and manner of selecting their representatives or spokesmen, and leads them to the office door of their employer with the legal authority to negotiate for their fellow employees. The Bill does not go beyond the office door.[4]

BARGAINING PROVISIONS IN THE WAGNER ACT

Exactly what Congress had in mind when it placed the bargaining provisions in the Act is unclear. It is obvious that the Board would not have the authority enjoyed in some countries of concluding that, because a particular standard or practice had been adopted by a majority of firms in a particular industry, an employer would have to agree to a union request for a similar clause. It seems similarly obvious that the Board was intended to "go beyond the door." The interesting questions are how far and in what way. Considering that one of the stated purposes of the Act was to raise wages and increase the purchasing power of workers, and Senator Wagner's strong belief in the necessity of increasing the bargaining power of the workers, it is not unlikely that the em-

[3] Senate Report 573, p. 3, 74th Cong. 1st Sess. 1935.
[4] Senator Walsh's statement is from 79th Cong. Rec. 7660 (1935).

ployer's duty to bargain was seen as giving unions a positive assist. In other words, the hand of the employer would be weakened, and that of the union strengthened.

If in fact this section was intended to strengthen unions, could it have any meaning, unless the Board was empowered to reject the soundness of an employer's offer? Viewed one way, the answer is in the negative. In a situation where union sentiment is strong, there are advantages to the employer in dealing with a certified union. His position is more easily communicated to the workers, and there is less chance of wildcat activity, etc. It is only when the union is very weak that the employer refuses to bargain at all or refuses to bargain on some issue. If relative bargaining power is the sole determinant of the content of the negotiated contract, it would seem that the outcome should be the same, regardless of whether the employer made a unilateral decision or made it in conjunction with a union in a bargaining context he completely dominated.

The same arguments would apply to a situation where the employer refused to bargain only upon a single issue. He would seldom choose an issue upon which the employees were strongly united, unless he wanted a strike. Or, is there something within the process of negotiation itself which would strengthen a weak union? In other words, in situations where the union is weak, will the terms be any more favorable to the membership if they are dictated by the employer in bargaining rather than being unilaterally promulgated by him? If one visualizes the process of bargaining as taking place with perfect information on all sides, then only the single solution given by relative power is possible. Then, mathematical computations of the willngness and ability of both sides to obtain their goals can be placed into a computer and a contract written. This, of necessity, neglects reality. Negotiations do not take place with anything resembling perfect knowledge. The employer has but a hazy guess of his expected permanently lost sales, and the union members may not know their wives' willingness to tolerate them at home and underfoot during a strike. Too, one's expectations prior to negotiation can be completely changed by the process of bargaining.

The 1959 steel strike is a good example of the effect of the events of negotiations upon the substance of union-management behavior. Here was a situation where, prior to the start of the negotiations, there was general agreement that the union's membership would not give strong support to a strike for higher wages. It was also well known that the principal consumers of steel had acquired large stockpiles as a hedge against a lengthy strike. The wise readers of tea leaves said that there would be no strike or at worst a token strike with a reasonable settlement. Into this situation the employers brought a demand for a change in the Section 2-b clause, which dealt with the determination of working rules and practices. The demand which the companies felt to be quite reasonable for an increased ability to make unilateral changes in contexts, where technological change had altered the old arrangements, was interpreted by the members of the union as a direct threat to hard-won gains. The result was our longest steel strike in history.

From this it seems reasonable to conclude that if an employer approaches the prospect of initial bargaining with a newly certified union with an enlarged fear of its cost, and the employees lack confidence in their ability to deal with an unwilling employer, forced negotiation will serve to strengthen the hand of the union. It will do so by increasing the members' confidence and by reducing the imagined threat in the mind of the company. Viewed in this light, a rather generous interpretation of the rationalization which the authors of the Wagner Act did not provide, it seems clear that the positive requirement to bargain fitted the purposes of the Act as seen by its sponsor.

REQUIREMENTS OF THE DUTY TO BARGAIN

The law requires that the employer and, with the passage of the Taft-Hartley Act, the union bargain in good faith over terms of employment. Cases arising under this duty can be divided into those associated with the three concepts of "bargain," "good faith," and "terms of employment." Our division will not necessarily follow the statements in Board and court decisions, for these exhibit a tendency to make rather widespread use of the term "good faith" when in point of fact it may well be immaterial to the content of the decision.

"To Bargain"

Meeting and Participation. Certain requirements are so obvious that they are found in NLB and old NLRB decisions and were incorporated into the Act in 1947. The employer or union must be willing to meet, and to reduce the agreed upon contract to writing, etc. Even here there are violations. A union was certified at the Aldora Mills[5] in Barnesville, Georgia, on April 23, 1946. It could not arrange an initial bargaining session with the company until August 27, 1946. Sixteen fruitless sessions over seven months led to an NLRB hearing. Four years after certification a circuit court upheld the Board's refusal to bargain decision, but the union had ceased to exist.

A more interesting employer dodge was that perfected by *Montgomery Ward.*[6] There the company negotiators listened politely to the demands by the union, declined to agree, and sat back quietly awaiting the next demand. Their position was that, since they did not wish anything from the union, the union had to submit a contract to them with which the company could agree. They thereby defined bargaining as consisting of recognizing the authority of the union, participating in discussions to avoid mutual misunderstanding, and entering into binding agreements upon those items, if any, upon which they could mutually agree. The Court, quite correctly it would seem, felt that the Ward concept should be broadened to include active participation in the deliberations,

---

[5] *Aldora Mills,* 79 NLRB 1 (1948); 22 LRRM 370; enforced 180 F. 2d 580 (1950); 25 LRRM 2530.
[6] *Montgomery Ward* v. *NLRB,* 133 F. 2d 676 (1943); 12 LRRM 508.

indicating a present intention to find a basis for agreement. In other words, a sincere effort to reach a common ground had to be made.

Providing Information. In part, the process of negotiation consists of an exchange of information. Does it follow that one party, the sole holder of certain facts, must supply them to the other upon request? And if so, at what cost and with what degree of veracity? In the *Truitt Manufacturing Company*[7] case, the company claimed it could give no more than the 2½-cent wage increase which it had offered and that it could not afford the 10 cents which the union demanded, because its wages were above the average of its competitors. The company also mentioned its precarious financial position, saying that it would break them to increase wages by 10 cents. The Board held it to be settled law that, when an employer seeks to justify not granting a wage increase because of economic inability, good faith bargaining requires it to attempt to substantiate its position. The Court of Appeals was not convinced, feeling that "to bargain in good faith does not require that the bargainer must substantiate by proof, statements made by him in the course of the bargaining." Mr. Justice Black, speaking for the Supreme Court, said that good faith bargaining requires honest claims and that, if an argument were important enough to be present in the give and take of bargaining, it was important enough to require some sort of proof. It is perhaps unfortunate that the words "good faith" appear in a matter such as this, for what does it imply for the role of the honest bluff, a tactic generally considered legitimate even if "all's fair in love, war, and collective bargaining" is not? Perhaps it would be more in keeping with reason and logic to set as a requirement of bargaining that a party be required to furnish reasonable information if known, provided it is the sole reasonably available source for such data. Clearly there will have to be limits. An example is when data which the employer maintains only for multiple groups are re-

[7] *NLRB* v. *Truitt Manufacturing Co.*, 351 U.S. 149 (1956); 38 LRRM 2042.

quested for a single group and where subdivision of the data would be quite expensive.

Unilateral Action.   Can it be bargaining if, on a subject upon which negotiation is required, one party takes unilateral action? It is clear that a 7-cent wage increase the day before negotiations begin would be illegal. The more interesting questions arise when, after extensive discussion and bargaining, the parties are unable to agree. Can the employer institute a change? A partial answer came in *Crompton-Highland Mills,*[8] where about two weeks after making a final offer of up to 1½ cents, rejected by the union, the company granted increases of 2 to 6 cents an hour. The authorities took a dim view of this behavior. Two questions can be raised: one is the time factor, and the second is the improvement of the wage offer. What, for example, would have happened if all of the workers had struck and then gradually returned to work? Could the employer have put into effect his last offer, a better offer? Suppose that historically nonunit personnel had received any improvements contained in the new contracts. Once impasse with the union is reached, what effect would the employer's putting into effect his last and best offer for these personnel have? Here, too, the Court tied the company's action to good faith, though the statutory requirement to bargain would appear to be the key.

The question of unilateral action has also arisen in cases dealing with the right to subcontract, and to close plants, etc. In these cases the companies have taken actions relating to subcontracting or closing plants without consulting the union, only to be told later that these were areas of mandatory bargaining (see the discussion under Subjects of Bargaining).

Finally, is it legal to fiddle while Rome burns? Can a party engage in good faith bargaining in the conference room and embark on a course of otherwise legal actions outside that will subject it to charges of bad faith bargaining? It is difficult to see anything wrong in such conduct, for if a union is free to strike, it would

[8] *NLRB* v. *Crompton-Highland Mills,* 337 U S. 217 (1949); 24 LRRM 2088.

seem to be free to engage in lesser forms of nonwork. In the principal case on this point, the *Insurance Agents*,[9] the NLRB initially found bad faith. There, after the contract expired, the Prudential Insurance Company agents began a program of not attending meetings, being in the office but not working, refusing to write new policies, etc. The NLRB decided that these actions were inconsistent with good faith attempts to write a new contract, since an impasse had not been reached. The Supreme Court reversed the Board's decision, explaining that this implied too much control over the method of bargaining and went beyond congressional intent in the area. Three of the judges, while approving the specific decision, disapproved of its implication that harassing tactics, regardless of their character, never constituted bad faith. They would have limited the decision to the specific facts of the case.

Good Faith

In 1948, in North Carolina, the ABC Mills employees voted in the XYZ Workers Union. The employer agreed to negotiate—or did he? He met with the union, but he is said to have bragged that XYZ would never get a contract. Among other things, he insisted that he would not accept a proposed grievance procedure, nor would he agree to arbitration, and he wished the union to be financially responsible for any unauthorized strikes which might occur. A year after certification, with no contract yet signed, a decertification election was held and lost by the union. Such actions might well have been the basis for a finding of a lack of good faith, in the sense that the one party had no intention of reaching agreement. As can be guessed, a belief that one party is unwilling to come to any sort of agreement might be inferred from a number of actions, including the dilatory tactics mentioned above, a refusal to discuss a subject unless a party's position is accepted, and obviously insincere negotiating. Reflection, however, should suggest that the insincere company could probably avoid the "good faith" trap by a program of hard bargaining. In other words, the employer would

[9] *NLRB v. Insurance Agents,* 361 U.S. 477 (1959); 48 LRRM 2704.

meet with the union at reasonable terms, fully discuss each issue, but always insist upon contractual conditions which would be completely unacceptable to the union. The question of the substance of the employer's offer is, then, an important one, even if the intent of judging its acceptability is not to use it to force increased wages, etc. My reading of congressional history has suggested to me that Congress intended that the substance should be judged. In a very, very limited way, it has been. In the celebrated *Reed and Prince*[10] case, Judge Magruder, speaking for the First Circuit Court, upheld a Board decision and said:

. . . If an employer can find nothing whatever to agree to in an ordinary current day contract submitted to him, or in some of the union's minor related requests, and if the employer makes not a single serious proposal meeting the union at least part way . . . this is at least some evidence of bad faith.

The above case was an exaggerated one dealing with a first contract in which the employer found himself unable to agree to the inclusion of language taken directly from the Act itself. Where the situation has been one involving the renewal of a contract, the stand taken has been less firm and positions of hard bargaining have been allowed. To date, the clearest example is the Bethlehem Steel Shipbuilding Company,[11] whose initial proposals contained in a white paper, were never relaxed. Once an impasse in bargaining was reached, the company unilaterally changed the seniority of union officers and parts of the grievance procedure. The trial examiner held that the company only violated the law in demanding that the union agree that each individual personally sign his grievances. The Board found additional violations in the post impasse change in the seniority of union officers and the change in the grievance system. It agreed with the trial examiner that it

[10] *NLRB* v. *Reed and Prince*, 205 F. 2d 131 at 133 (1953); 32 LRRM 2225 at 2228, cert. den. 346 U.S. 887.
[11] *NLRB* v. *Bethlehem Steel Company*, 133 NLRB 1347 (1961); 49 LRRM 1016; supplemented 136 NLRB 1500 (1962); 50 LRRM 1016: reversed 320 F. 2d 615 (1963); 53 LRRM 2878 cert. den. 375 U.S. 984.

did not represent a situation of overall bad faith bargaining. Upon review, the Third Circuit Court of Appeals sent the case back to the Board. The Court held that the company's demand that each employee personally sign his own grievance was not a mandatory subject for bargaining. Given this, the impasse in the negotiations resulted from the company's bad faith bargaining when it insisted upon a nonmandatory subject and hence not only were the unilateral changes illegal, but the strike itself was caused by the bad faith bargaining of the company. With the recent revival of hard bargaining, General Electric being a good example, the problems raised by judgments of substantive positions will become of greater significance.

Subjects of Bargaining

In 1939, on the basis that it was not a proper subject for bargaining, the NLRB decided that an employer could not condition his agreement to a contract upon his insistence that the union organize other firms in the industry. From this has flowed two increasing lists of subjects, those which are nonmandatory, and those which are mandatory, subject to bargaining because they fall within the area of "wages, hours, and other terms and conditions of employment." As this book is written, perhaps these things do not sound surprising, but at the time of their announcement the fact that mandatory subjects included things like pensions and Christmas bonuses was quite shocking to many employers. Of late, the list of required subjects has been expanded into job security concerns like subcontracting, relocating the plant, closing a plant, etc.

The NLRB's concern with subcontracting and the duty to bargain began, for practical purposes, in 1962 when it decided the *Town and Country Manufacturing Company*[12] and *Fibreboard Paper Products Corporation*[13] cases. In *Town and Country*, one

[12] NLRB v. *Town and Country Manufacturing Co.*, 136 NLRB 1022, (1963); 49 LRRM 1918: enforced 316 F. 2d 846, 53 LRRM 2054.

[13] NLRB v. *Fibreboard Paper Products Corp.*, 138 NLRB 550 (1962); 51 LRRM 110: enforced 322 F. 2d 411 (1963); 53 LRRM 2667: cert. granted 375 U.S. 963 (1963).

month after the drivers voted in a union, the company subcontracted its hauling and terminated the drivers' employment. The company gave economic factors as the reason. The Board found that, in addition, the company was motivated by anti-union motives. The company was ordered to re-establish its old operation. In *Fibreboard* the anti-union motive was not present. Near the end of a contract the company decided it could save money if it contracted its entire maintenance operation to an outside firm. The company then told the union that it would be useless to negotiate a new agreement. The NLRB held that it was a violation of the Act for the firm to subcontract the work without first bargaining with the union. This decision was made when the case was reconsidered by the Board, the initial decision being that the company's action did not violate the law.

The reconsidered opinion was upheld by the Second Circuit Court of Appeals, then accepted for Supreme Court determination in its October 1964 term, and subsequently upheld.

Company spokesmen have viewed these two cases with alarm. They are seen as: (1) circumscribing management's ability to make major business decisions; and (2) greatly enlarging the area of joint decision-making. It is still too early to know whether the employers' fears are valid. In terms of normal business operations, both cases are atypical. One involved an anti-union motive and the other, the complete destruction of the entire bargaining relationship. The true import of this mandatory subject will become apparent when cases in which the firms are involved in numerous "make or buy" decisions are decided.

There is an important legal difference between the categories classified as mandatory and nonmandatory. If one party raises a mandatory subject, the other must bargain, and a party's position can be insisted upon to the point of impasse. A voluntary or nonmandatory subject may be raised but the other party does not have to bargain over it, and, most importantly, it cannot be the subject which precipitates a strike. Another seeming difference is that the growing list of mandatory subjects is made up typically of concerns which managements had believed were strictly within their control, while those declared voluntary have most often been subjects raised by management. While some of this difference may be accounted for by the approach of the Board, the best explanation lies in the inherent elasticity of the term "conditions of employment," the internal political need of union officials to "lead," but most importantly, changing economic conditions.

There are some clauses whose inclusion in a contract would be illegal. The closed shop would be an example. A party can obviously not insist upon the inclusion of such a clause or enforce it if it is voluntarily agreed upon. Of greater significance are those clauses where the insistence upon a particular course of action is held to be an unfair labor practice, even though the general area is clearly mandatory and the wording which is insisted upon is not illegal if the other party was willing to accept it. An excellent example is the recent *Erie Resistor*[14] case, in which the company insisted that replacements hired during a strike were to have 20 years of seniority plus whatever they gained from being employed by Erie. The same "gift" was also granted to employees who gave up the strike and returned to work. The company claimed the move was made necessary by the fact that a number of its employees were on layoff. One needed about eight years of seniority in order to have been employed at the time of strike. The decision by the Supreme Court was that the right of the employer to permanently replace strikers had to give way to the right of the employee to be able to exercise those rights which were guaranteed to him by the Act. This raises the intriguing question of the legality of the clause granting super-seniority even if the union had voluntarily agreed to it. If the union had agreed to the clause, could an individual employee have gone to the NLRB and had it declared illegal because it bargained away one of his rights under the Act?

If not the classic case, one of the most important of the mandatory-nonmandatory cases is *Borg-Warner*[15] (1958). In *Borg-*

[14] *NLRB* v. *Erie Resistor Co.*, 373 U.S. 221 (1963); 53 LRRM 2121.
[15] *NLRB* v. *Wooster Division of Borg-Warner Corp.*, 356 U.S. 342 (1958); 42 LRRM 2034.

Warner the company insisted as a condition for its entering into a collective bargaining agreement that: (1) rather than the international union which had been certified as the representative by the NLRB, the local union would be the recognized bargaining agent; and (2) before a strike could be called the union had to submit the employer's final offer to a vote in which nonunion members as well as union members of the unit could vote. The union would not agree and a 1½-month strike ensued. Later, the union settled and the contract included the company's two demands.

The certification question is minor and need not concern us. The Board and the Courts had little trouble agreeing that it was a nonmandatory subject. Indeed, it really should be classed as an illegal subject, since certification is a right of the NLRB and not of the parties. On the company's insistence on the ballot condition, a divided (5–4) Supreme Court upheld the Board and in the process overturned the lower court which had ruled for the company. It held that it was a violation of good faith to insist that a contract include a nonmandatory subject. In doing so it upheld a Board decision that the company's ballot demand was a "per se" violation of the Act, thus making this behavior one of the few "per se" rules approved by the high Court. Since in the course of events the company had accepted the 1½-month strike rather than yield and had thereby won its point, the import of the decision was to take away from the company contract clauses which had been won in fair combat.

SHOULD THE DUTY TO BARGAIN BE LIMITED?

Cases like *Borg-Warner* have given rise to increased concern, by many students of labor, that the duty to bargain in good faith requirement is putting the government more and more into a situation in which it does not belong, and that parties are using it as a form of private game playing rather than using the time to settle their differences. One of the clearest statements is contained in the admirable *The Public Interest in National Labor Policy*:

> Parties have been told that they must bargain in good faith, and elaborate tests have been devised in an attempt to determine "objectively" whether the proper subjective attitude prevails. The limitations and artificiality of such tests are apparent, and the possibilities of evasion are almost limitless. In the light of the realities of the bargaining situations, distinctions between matters that are subject to "mandatory bargaining" and those that are not have a hollow ring. Basically, it is unrealistic to expect that by legislation "good faith" can be brought to the bargaining table. . . . The subjects to be covered by the bargaining, the procedures to be followed, the nuances of strategy involving the timing of a "best offer," the question of whether to re-open a contract during its term—such matters as these are best left to the parties themselves.[16]

Though the cited report does not provide an elaborate rationalization for its position, its authors' underlying reasons are not difficult to divine. In part, it represents a feeling that the requirement serves no great usefulness and that in such cases the less government interference the better. It also implies that parties "use" the Act and that its being so used is unwise or inappropriate. Lastly, there would appear to be a belief that it is somehow wrong for the implementation of the Act to reverse, as in *Borg-Warner*, the results of economic realities. We do not have the time to engage in an extended discussion of this, though it is an interesting and fruitful subject. As the study group recognized, though not explicitly, much of what they objected to was not necessarily tied up in "good faith" since the mere duty to bargain over terms and conditions would let most of their dragons into the nursery. Also, from the point of view suggested here, the use of the Act for private games is a fact of life not necessarily to be deplored, unless of course the wrong side is winning. Beyond that, it is perhaps

[16] An Independent Study Group, *The Public Interest in National Labor Policy*, Committee for Economic Development 1960, p. 82.

easiest to evaluate the committee's position by considering the alternatives.

One alternative would be to repeal the duty to bargain requirement. The practical import of this would be very close to the W*ard* case discussed earlier. If the employer wishes to deal with his employees, he must do so with the certified union. There would be nothing, however, to force him to deal with employees except to announce his employment terms. The impact of such a change cannot be predicted in detail. For the vast majority of current relationships it would not eliminate the bargaining process. Nor is it even clear that it would have a very great effect among the newly organizing, for even the employer who is very powerful relative to the union probably stands to gain something by formally dealing with a union. The real import would result from shifts in bargaining power growing out of the changed bargaining tactics which would be induced. To remove the bargaining requirement goes further than the authors of the report wished to go. They are in favor of getting rid of the unimportant things. One suggestion in this vein, to eliminate decisions over the content of the negotiations, was proposed by Stanley Jacks. It would be accomplished by adding the following to the statute:

> Nor shall such obligation limit the right of either party to insist upon the inclusion of any lawful provision as a condition of agreement.[17]

This would make mute the sometimes seemingly artificial boundary between mandatory and nonmandatory classes. To the extent that some of the nonmandatory subjects are demanded by the company for good purpose, such as the willingness of the union to post a performance bond, it would probably be a desirable change. Good purpose implies that they wish it in the contract because of a fear of illegal strikes or because they feel that its cost will weaken the union. Yet, might not the demand's purpose be

---

[17] Stanley M. Jacks, "National Labor Policy and the Duty to Bargain Collectively," *Industrial Management Review* 3, Spring 1962, p. 59.

the prevention of a contract? In other words, will there still have to be a limit? The concept of "good faith," if it had not been dropped, might provide a limit—but what if this action were the sole proof of a lack of good faith? One step might be to add, after the word agreement, "provided that the party from whom the demand is made has the authority to fulfill the demand." This would allow the performance bond, and it would still leave illegal a demand from a certified local that the international be responsible for illegal strikes. It would also, of course, leave as a "condition of employment" the salaries of the management or the type of advertising campaigns which the companies used. Would those who view the current extension of mandatory subjects as "significantly narrowing the area of managerial discretion in operating the enterprises" be willing to go so far? Or is it somehow possible to limit what management must bargain about and at the same time open up union areas? An additional clause saying something to the effect that matters which do not have clear and direct impact upon the terms and conditions of employment would not be bargainable would at least protect management salaries from negotiations, even though it would not eliminate the subcontracting and plant close-downs as legitimate factors.

Were one to be true to the critics' suggestion that playing private games with the Act is somehow undesirable, one would have to curtail the right of unions to receive information. Yet, as has been suggested, for many issues the information supplied by the company is the only thing which allows bargaining. And what clause would distinguish between the necessary and the harassing demand for data? One could go on, but hopefully the trend is clear. It would seem wisest to recognize that if the duty to bargain is to mean anything other than dealing with the certified union if the employer deals with any representative of his employees, the parties will use the Act for private gain and that the addition of elaborate provisos is apt to be of no avail.

THE IMPACT OF THE DUTY TO BARGAIN
ON COLLECTIVE BARGAINING

During the fiscal years 1958 through 1962, companies engaged in 1008 violations of the duty to bargain section of the Act. Here a violation is defined as the informal settlement of a meritorious charge plus all decisions that were not subsequently reversed by a higher tribunal that a violation had occurred. In addition, fully half of the firms violated other sections of the Act, usually by engaging in illegal discharges. Of these 1008, 581 involved situations where there was no prior history of bargaining and 162 involved relationships which were less than 3 years old, though 145 had a bargaining history in excess of 11 years. The 1008 cases involved the issues listed in the table below.

TABLE 1.   NATURE OF VIOLATIONS IN DUTY TO
BARGAIN CASES, 1958–1962

Issue	Number of Cases[a]
Refusal to recognize the union	333
Refusal to sign contract	125
Unilateral action	299
Bad faith bargaining	344
Mandatory subject matter	35
Unit contested	69
Bypassing union	174
Refusal to supply information	106
Other	37

[a] Total may not sum to 1008 due to several issues per case.
SOURCE: Frank M. McCulloch, "The Consequences of NLRB Action on Good Faith Bargaining," a speech reported in *Daily Labor Report*, May 27, 1964, pp. D-1–D-6.

But what happened after the case was settled? Was behavior changed? Were contracts written? Were permanent relationships established? The 581 cases involving a first contract resulted in 300 contracts being entered into and 281, including 57 where the plant closed or moved, ended with no contract. The results are much better in the older relationships where the end result was a contract in 81 percent of the cases for relationships aged 3 to 10 years, and 90 percent in the over 11-years category. The probability that a contract will finally be signed diminishes with extended litigation. For new bargaining situations where the company did not move or did not go out of business and the violation was settled before reaching the Board, a contract was signed three out of four times. The three-in-four dropped to one-in-two if the case went to the Board and to one-in-three if it required a circuit court determination.

Another alternative method of grouping the data is by size of the bargaining unit. Looked at in this way, it appears that the failure to bargain is a small unit problem, for a majority of all violations were in units with less than 39 employees and the probability was twice as great that a violation would have occurred in a unit of 9 employees as it would had it occurred in a unit of 500 or more employees.

Informative as these data are, they still leave unresolved the question of the economic impact upon the firms of the Board's pronouncements in this area. There is no easy solution, for there are no research findings in this area.

SUMMARY

Despite the large number of court cases and the numerous categories like "mandatory," "illegal," "bad faith," etc., the duty to bargain requirement is conceptually very simple. The essence of the Wagner Act was that workers had a right to an organized role in determining their employment conditions. This placed two requirements upon the employer. One of these, encompassed in the duty to bargain, was to make meaningful the employee's right to codetermination of his wages, hours, etc. Obviously, this right can only be meaningful if the employer: (1) meets with the union; (2) supplies the union with information which would otherwise be unavailable; (3) does not try to undermine the union by dealing directly with employees or by granting improvements in working conditions directly to the employees; and (4) does not insist upon union agreement to provisions unrelated to employment conditions, etc. The list of specific do's and don't's could be continued at great length, but the import is clear. If an employer accepts the union's right to speak to the employees, then his actions are not apt to violate the law. If an employer is not willing to accept the legitimacy of the union's role, then whatever action or actions he utilizes in his attempt to lessen the union's influence will probably violate the duty to bargain.

Suggested Readings

Robben W. Fleming, "The Obligation to Bargain in Good Faith," a chapter in Joseph Shister, *et. al.*, *Public Policy and Collective Bargaining*, New York: Harper & Row, 1962.

Russell B. Smith, "The Evolution of the 'Duty to Bargain' Concept in American Law," *Michigan Law Review*, 39, May, 1941, pp. 1065–1088.

CHAPTER 7

The Chief Executive
and Dispute Settlement

In recent years the President of the United States has become involved in labor disputes running the gauntlet from the orchestra of the Metropolitan Opera and 1500 workers in an atomic energy plant to the industry-wide problems of the steel and railroad industries. Do these disputes share a common characteristic? Are there criteria which would indicate why these have been presidential emergencies, while similar ones have not been so considered?

CRITERIA FOR EMERGENCY DISPUTES

There are four general types of criteria which can be listed. These are economic, national defense, external political, and internal political or the convenience of the public. The most widely discussed in professional literature are the economic factors. One author has written that the product must be essential, the emergency imminent, and the impact truly national. This includes disputes involving products like coal and steel which are produced for a national market as well as industries like the railroads which produce for separate markets, but where bargaining is done on a nationwide basis. It would exclude electrical utilities where both markets and extent of bargaining are local or regional.

In addition to having a national effect, the product must be essential, that is, it must be without adequate substitutes in kind or in time. One would not include a nationwide strike of all the airlines because there are ample alternative means of transport. But a nationwide strike of local telephone companies (unless minimal operations could be maintained by supervisors) would be classed as an emergency because storage of telephone service is not possible and there are no adequate substitutes. By the criterion of substitutes, a strike in the long-distance portion of the telephone industry would not be considered to be an emergency, because of letters, the telegraph, messengers, etc. Lastly, the danger must be imminent or actual rather than prospective, transpiring only *if* the problem persisted long enough. In other words, if the use of pre-strike inventories and post-strike extra production meant that serious consequences would be felt only after a strike of 50 days, for example, then its classification as an emergency would be then and not when the strike first began.

The external political criterion is rather ill-defined. People who refer to it are usually concerned with the image of our society, way of life, and economic system as seen by the uncommitted nations of the world. The argument is that our image is tarnished by a seeming inability to prevent emergency strikes. After all, would the brakemen on the Moscow to Leningrad railroad strike? Why the other countries are not impressed by the obvious freedom associated with such situations is never made clear. Some strikes that might fit this definition would be the lengthy New York City newspaper strike of 1962–1963 and the comedy of errors associated with our efforts to have the nuclear ship *Savannah* show the flag of progress around the world. The *Savannah*, though owned by the federal government, was to be operated by a private firm. The engineers who were to operate the ship received special training at government expense. Then they demanded higher pay because of the increased knowledge required and the danger. An arbitration agreement to settle their strike which tied their wages to those of deck officers only compounded the situation. With regard to the newspaper strike, it was reported that a major public figure in South America had his view of the United States severely shaken. Following one of his speeches, he asked the American Ambassador how it had been received in the United States. After the Ambassador's reply was the question, "Ah yes, but what did the *Times* say?"

The area of national defense is easily the most difficult one to define, except during periods of general war like 1941–1945. Then almost any dispute was considered to be an emergency. In fact, the National War Labor Board asserted jurisdiction over a dispute involving the Brooklyn Y.M.C.A. For limited wars, like the Korean War, the proper definition would seem to involve the directness of the relationship between the production and its use in the combat theatre. Clearly this would include the production of ammunition, but what of steel mills? The 1952 steel strike between June 2 and July 24 was widely regarded at the time as, in the words of Secretary of Defense Robert Lovett, ". . . A national calamity that had damaged defense production more than the worst possible enemy bombing raid could have done."[1] Presidential advisor John Steelman reported that it would take one year to offset the effects of the steel shortage on defense production.

Actually, the strike appears to have had little if any discernible impact. The widely reported shortage in Korea of certain types of ammunition is not traceable to the strike and the *Washington Post* reported on September 5, 1952, that the delivery of tanks, guns, and ammunition reached a new peak in July of that year. A comparison might also be made between the 93 million tons of 1952 steel output with the 89 and 90 million ton production records in 1943 and 1944. Another defense criterion for indirect industries like steel in periods of limited and cold wars has been stated in a discussion of the 1952 steel strike by Harold Enarson:

[1] From *The Wall Street Journal*, July 25, 1952.

The ramifying effect of the strike on mobilization schedules was incalculable. Plainly, the result was to delay production of military end items which would have been badly needed in the event of *all-out* war. . . . It is no answer to say that the country survived. No one can measure the vulnerability to enemy attack or count the cost had we been plunged into war. [Emphasis added.][2]

But would not the same logic suggest that we should build next year's military items this year? It is this type of rationale that lies behind many of today's statements in favor of governmental intervention in current disputes involving defense production.

The final criterion is the internal political or the convenience of the public. Its most difficult aspect is that the public's anticipation of its lost convenience during the strike will probably be greater than its after-the-strike assessment of its lost convenience. Yet, it is the prestrike or early strike assessment which appears to have the greatest influence upon public officials. An excellent example was a local bus strike in Boston some years ago. Just prior to the strike and during its first days the papers were filled with editorials calling upon the governor to act and with stories giving details of the massive impact upon the public. The governor did not act, the dispute became involved in personalities, and it dragged on and on. When at last it was over, the same papers painted the governor as a hero for his intelligence and ability to stand up to foolish pressure.

Professional students of labor typically view this last criterion with disfavor. They would have the President side with the former director of the Federal Mediation and Conciliation Service, Cyrus Ching, who said that there never had been a real national emergency, and act accordingly. Their conclusion stems from the belief that a policy of too easy recourse to the intervention of government leads the parties, or certainly one of them, to try to use the government to gain ends they cannot secure from pure collective bargaining. This leads to a breakdown in the bargaining by the

[2] Harold L. Enarson, "The Politics of an Emergency Dispute: Steel 1952,' in Irving Bernstein, *et al.* (eds.), *Emergency Disputes and National Policy*, New York: Harper & Row, 1955, p. 72.

parties as they await their cues from Washington. The end product has been graphically outlined by John Perry Horlacher:

> In the long run, a free society can only enslave itself if it values more highly the conveniences, comfort, and material blessings of an uninterrupted flow of goods and services than it does its fundamental liberties.[3]

In defense of the public convenience, it should be recalled that the majority of employment relationships are determined outside of collective bargaining, that large numbers of employees are explicitly denied the right to strike (governmental), and that only a small portion of all workers covered by collective bargaining are apt to be involved in emergency type disputes. Considering this, it is not surprising that there are strong political pressures in favor of a convenience rather than an emergency standard, nor does it seem to be such an inappropriate one.

The compelling conclusion of the experts is that most interventions into labor-management strife on the grounds that otherwise a national emergency would exist are not justified except perhaps by political considerations. It should be recognized, however, that Presidents exist in a world of politics. Thus, the experts might serve a more useful function were they to spend more time carrying out studies designed to inform a President of the political costs which would be incurred if the President adopted alternative responses to certain disputes rather than spending time developing elaborate explanations for why particular strikes were not national emergencies, and not worthy of presidential intervention.

ALTERNATIVE POLICIES

In 1947 two men, Senator Robert A. Taft and Professor Sumner Slichter of Harvard University, proposed and saw enacted, emergency strike legislation premised upon the concept of uncertainty.

[3] John Perry Horlacher, "A Political Science View of National Emergency Disputes," *The Annals of the American Academy of Political and Social Science*, 333, January, 1961, p. 86.

Both felt that if the parties were unsure of the outcome of governmental intervention, they would be less likely to seek its use. In both cases the results have not been those which were foreseen or hoped for by the authors.

Taft-Hartley

The Taft-Hartley law provisions which allow the President to secure an 80-day injunction against what he believes to be an emergency strike have been used 21 times in the last 16 years, but only 14 times in the last 15. In 6 of them the strike was resumed after the end of the 80-day period. A few industries account for most of the observations. Five were in atomic energy (one of these was a metal fabricator), 3 in coal, 2 in maritime, and 6 in longshoring. If, on the grounds that they involve very different contexts, strikes in 1948–1949 as well as those of the Korean War are excluded, the Act has been used ten times, with two thirds of its use confined to two industries, atomic energy and longshoring. If emergency situations are regrouped to include, in addition to those in which the Taft-Hartley Act machinery was used, some like the missile-sites, airline, railroad, and aerospace disputes of the early 1960s which were handled by *ad hoc* means, the more recent emergency disputes fall into two broad categories. The categories are those involving firms whose output is purchased almost entirely by the government and those which have involved the painful process of reducing the number of employees required for specific jobs. Thus, if one seeks solutions other than (better than) those contained in Taft-Hartley, they should be designed to deal primarily with disputes having these two characteristics rather than those of some "typical" but mythical emergency strike.

Should a new method of dealing with these situations be sought? The record of the last ten years might seem favorable to the retention of the Taft-Hartley Act procedure. Only two of the disputes in which it was used, both involving longshoring, have resulted in lost production after the injunction was lifted, and then for only 11 and 33 days respectively. But listen to a Taft act critic. The emergency disputes section of the Taft-Hartley Act has not worked at all well and the statistical test just cited is inappropriate. It is inappropriate because for most Presidents the use of the Taft-Hartley law is a last step. A President is much more apt to turn to an *ad hoc* solution as did President Kennedy in the missile-sites and aerospace disputes. The usefulness of the *ad hoc* solution is that it can often provide a method for attempting to assist in the settlement of the dispute rather than merely giving the parties another 80 days in which they may talk if they wish.

Wisely or not, the emergency disputes section does not provide machinery to assist in settlement because its author did not intend it to. Senator Taft strongly believed that if the parties couldn't settle after 80 days in the eye of the public, then Congress and only Congress should fashion a remedy for the particular strike. In view of congressional inaction in the 1963 railroad case, Taft's reliance upon its wisdom may seem ill-founded. In some ways the critics are correct. Strikes are only settled through the operation of economic or political pressure or increased information on intents and costs. The Taft-Hartley procedure specifically affects none of these. Whether political pressures similar to the extralegal ones now used or economic ones similar to those of a regular strike should be specifically written into legislation is debatable. Most professional students and other critics seem to favor some kind of pressure. In fact, their most common proposal is for a "choice of procedures," and this takes us back to Professor Slichter.

Slichter Act

In the same year that Congress passed the Taft-Hartley Act, the Great and General Court of the Commonwealth of Massachusetts passed a state emergency disputes law which was based upon the recommendations of a commission headed by Professor Slichter. This law covering disputes in the production and distribution of food, fuel, water, electric light and power, gas, or hospital or medical services, allowed the governor, if he found an endangerment of the health or safety of any community, to require the parties to appear before a moderator to show cause why it should not go to voluntary arbitration, or to submit the dispute to an arbitration board. If these didn't work, voluntary arrangements could be made to continue complete or partial service, or failing this, the facility could be seized. The law was used twice in 1948 and four times in 1953. The advantages supposedly were that the uncertainty of the method of governmental intervention would preclude either party from using it to gain an extra advantage. In this it does not appear to have been successful. Over the years it tended to be pushed more and more to the ultimate sanction of seizure, which apparently favored the unions in the particular cases. Its use was then discontinued. The utility industry was one in which it was widely used. Changed methods of operation, as in the switch from manufactured to natural gas have, in recent years, allowed utility supervisors to maintain satisfactory service in the face of prolonged walkouts. This and the changing political climate within the state have made the law inoperative since 1953.

Current Proposals

The principal alternative to the Taft-Hartley Act method is probably the already mentioned "choice of procedures" involving different final measures and including the specific right to do nothing. Why this proposal has been so favorably received is somewhat difficult to understand, especially the feature of taking no action. Nothing now forces a President to act, and in some ways it is difficult to understand how having the specific right not to act will change the situation. (My Friends and Fellow Citizens, the dispute in the ABC industry is a national emergency, millions are starving, yet I shall do nothing believing that since all past strikes have ended, this one will too.) Of course this is too strong and one will never hear such a speech. Too, a President who did not wish to become involved in a specific dispute might well be strengthened if he could refer to a statute which stated that professionals in the field and in Congress agreed that one alternative in situations like these was to do nothing. Yet, as should be clear from the discussion of criteria and the industries and times in which it has been used, the actions of Presidents seem to have been dictated by their views of the public interest or the politically correct decision. Legislation or not, these will almost always push for intervention. Nor is it clear how a federal choice of procedures will avoid the problem faced in Massachusetts, of being pushed toward the ultimate sanction by whichever party believed it would benefit from it. This could be avoided if there were two ultimate sanctions, only one of which would be helpful to a single party, for example, seizure and compulsory arbitration. Even this may completely ignore political reality, as an examination of the failure of President Kennedy to give his full and unqualified support to the recommendations of the Presidential Railroad Commission in the rail dispute of 1963 would indicate.

To avoid a national railroad strike and hopefully to assist in the solution of a bargaining impasse, President Eisenhower appointed a 15-man Presidential Railroad Commission. President Kennedy reappointed 14 of the members and named a new chairman to replace one who had resigned. The Commission's task was to make recommendations, especially on the work rules issues, and hopefully to find some basis upon which the private parties could settle. The final report was written by the five neutral members and accepted by the five management representatives. The union representatives rejected the report and began an immediate and vocal attack against its recommendations. The President, apparently for political reasons, chose a publicly noncommittal position, though privately he is said to have strongly urged the unions to accept, at least in principle, most of the recommendations.

Perhaps the most widely recommended ultimate sanction, and the one with the poorest reputation among professionals in the field, is compulsory arbitration. The arguments against it are:

1. If one party, particularly the union, doesn't like the award, it has other ways, like slowdowns, to enforce its point of view. The rule book slowdown of the British Postal Workers is an excellent

example. There they merely observed every rule in their book of rules, like finding a legal parking place at railroad stations instead of double parking. The results were mounting bags of mail in post offices and a population both annoyed and amused.

2. The system has a poor record where it has been tried on a mass scale. This point must be stated with caution. It has operated since the turn of the century in New Zealand and Australia. In both, its role has been constructive, though in neither country has it completely eliminated strikes.

3. It is politically unacceptable to most of the parties in the United States, especially unions.

4. The parties don't bargain but await the decision of the Board. This is especially true if both believe that the Board would give them something more than their last recorded offer.

There are counterarguments that would seem to have some validity, especially if the question of whether Congress would pass a compulsory arbitration law is omitted. No one proposes that compulsory arbitration should be applied generally, so that experience in countries where it is widely used may be inappropriate. There is little evidence that contract solutions imposed by *ad hoc* means are more efficient than those of a more formal system. Recourse to nonprivate settlements would only be encouraged if it became easier to obtain access to the Arbitration Board than it is to obtain the use of *ad hoc* Boards today. In addition, the system might work better if the parties, in conjunction with those whose earlier mediation attempts had failed, were required to rank their outstanding differences in terms of their relative importance. The Arbitration Board would then decide the most important item and then give the negotiations back to the parties. If they still could not complete the contract, the Board would decide the next item and so on. Whether such a practice would help is hard to say. It is not unreasonable, though, to believe that, if in the 1963 railroad dispute, the suggestion of the President's Railroad Commission on the fireman issue had been an arbitration award, the parties could have then found some agreement on the rest of their outstanding differences, though when this was done more than a year later the results were hardly encouraging. In a similar way, in the 1959 steel dispute, a decision to send the Section 2-b proposal to lower levels for study of the exact problems which the companies faced in the various plants would probably have allowed the parties to complete their contract.

Seizure and the breakup of industry-wide bargaining have little to recommend them. Seizure provides no means of settlement unless the government is allowed to change the conditions of employment and, if this is to be the case, it might as well be compulsory arbitration. The breaking up of unions may or may not have advantages in the general area of union power; it clearly goes way beyond the requirements of the national emergency problem. A dark horse among solutions, but becoming more popular all the time, is the suggestion for partial operation. Its advantages are manifold. It provides the public with sufficient service to avoid the emergency, but still leaves substantial economic pressure upon the parties. It may well have merit and at least deserves further investigation of how it might work out in specific disputes.

Partial operation has two principal weaknesses as well as one minor weakness. Basically, it stems from a concept of national emergency strikes arising under the economic or national defense criteria. In the real world these are unimportant compared to the internal political criterion. Consequently, if the partial strike really eased the public convenience, it could well provide so much production that the economic pressure which was left over would be insignificant. Of perhaps greater importance is the question of how the limited production is allocated. A study made following the 1959 steel strike indicated that a partial operation of the steel industry to provide for defense needs would have been possible if the full range of the operated mills would have been utilized. It did not indicate what should have been done with the civilian goods thus produced. Could they be sold to the highest bidder? One automobile company misjudged the situation more than its competitors and had a much smaller steel stockpile. Should it have been bailed out of its unforeseen difficulties? The question of profits and wages earned is not a problem; they would either be shared by the parties or the pressure of whipsawing would soon force settlement. The minor weakness is that this method would shift the power balance between union and company, a thing supporters of most of the proposals would like to avoid.

The partial strike is akin to the play strike—a widely discussed but apparently highly impractical proposal made some ten or more years ago. There are a number of different formal proposals, but their principles are alike. The parties would continue to produce, the company would lose a portion of its profits, and the workers would lose a portion of their wages. The object would be to create pressures upon the parties equal to, and of similar relative magnitude to, the pressures of a regular strike, though of a lower level, and at the same time impose no loss upon the public. If not the most practical, at least it is an interesting suggestion and the working out of details and attempt to counterbalance its weaknesses is an instructive exercise. The principal problem is obviously that, to be effective, it would require case-by-case determination of the forfeits, and with less effort, the strike might be settled.

GOVERNMENT KEPT INDUSTRIES AND FEATHERBEDS

It was noted that a majority of recent disputes in which the government became involved were those where the bulk of industry's output was purchased by the government or where there was an attempt to abolish particular jobs. If there is a better formal solution than that now used, it would seem to be one that had particular applicability to these two classes. The dramatic rise in the proportion of gross national product represented by the governmental sector has not been paralleled by an equivalent rise in governmental production, especially of tangible goods. In part this has meant that a greater percentage of the output of all firms is produced for the government, a factor that probably has little importance for labor relations. It has also meant that for certain industries, the government has become the dominant customer and, in some cases, the principal supplier of capital. Viewed in some ways, this too should make little difference to the parties' private collective bargaining. Certainly it should have no greater impact than that which similar buyer-seller relationships have in other businesses. There are, however, certain differences in the quasi-governmental industries which may (probably) mean that the buyer will play a much more meaningful role. One is the monopsony character of the purchaser. In ordinary business relationships the supplier can and usually does sell to several firms. Compared to ordinary situations, the uniqueness of the product produced and the facilities required means that the implied ability of a buyer to shift suppliers in the advent of a strike does not exist. Lastly, and perhaps most important, the national defense character of the majority of the output tends to invite an earlier and keener governmental concern than would be true in the case of, say, a pin manufacturer. In other words, while it is perfectly possible for the government to treat disputes in quasi-governmental enterprises as strictly private ones, the realities of the situation suggest that this policy is not apt to develop. If not, what then?

An obvious alternative would be to make the government a formal party to the bargain. It could also be left to informal and *ad hoc* solutions, like the committee formed to mediate the jurisdictional disputes which plagued the missile-sites, the special fact-finding and mediating boards set up for the aero-space disputes, or the Presidential Railroad Commission. The suggestion of government participation as a formal partner has been made for other situations where some have felt the bargaining to have a degree of public interest, which, in their eyes, has been unrepresented by the private parties. Certainly the suggestion of a formal role for the government has merit, if for no other reason than that if intervention is probable, it might as well begin early. The principal weakness becomes obvious as consideration is given to the outcome of tri-party bargaining over a bilateral agreement. In this case, because of its power of the purse, even if the company and union combined against it, the sole purchaser could prevail. The end result is that the government would end up setting the principal terms of the agreement. An example might be the subsidized maritime industry. Since the federal subsidy involves the difference between United States labor costs and foreign ones, many observers feel the companies have allowed wage rates to rise much more rapidly than would have been the case with a different form of subsidy. A possible alternative would be for the government to privately inform the companies of the total increase in all costs which would be tolerated or to grant the companies some type of credits if cost increases were kept within certain types of bounds. Even these alternatives, if seriously considered, would mean that it would be in the union's best interest to push until the government formally intervenes and makes explicit recommendations.

There are then only two alternatives. One is to treat the area the same way that the rest of the private sector is treated, and to recognize that the true test of national defense needs makes intervention unnecessary except in periods of general war or the limited period leading up to war. September of 1938 would be an example of the latter, but what does one do with Mr. Chamberlain? The second is for the government to formally recognize its own role and to treat the quasi-governmental corporations in the same way that true governmental corporations like the TVA are treated. The latter suggestion would mean that industries and unions, in conjunction with the government, would be encouraged to develop a set of other firms by whose working conditions they could gauge their own. This would allow the employees to keep up, but not to lead in the development of improved wages and employment practices. The role of an extra-legal emergency board, if one were ever needed, would be to ascertain whether the correct interpretation was being made of the working conditions chosen as standard, or to alter the standard. But, experience with TVA and other governmental operations suggests that such arrangements should require little outside assistance. For nonwage items, the standard would seem to have to be governmental rather than private employment. Thus in the aerospace dispute of a few years ago, the intemperate remarks of the Wallen Board on the company's unwillingness to grant the union request for a union shop arrangement appear somewhat out of context with the Administration's refusal when it issued its executive order implementing collective bargaining in the federal service to grant similar status to its own employees. Here the principle is not so much whether the union shop is good or bad, but that there should be consistency.

The other major type of dispute which has involved the President is one of the most difficult aspects of the labor scene—disputes over the content of specific jobs or featherbedding (to use a popular but misused word). In some instances these problems have been more difficult than they might have been. One reason has been the continuing high rate of unemployment which has made the prospects of alternative jobs dimmer. A second has been the decline in available jobs in manufacturing relative to the rest of the economy. A third is the general lack of correspondence between areas, firms, and skills of the lost jobs and those where new jobs are developing. A fourth reason is that in some instances the job change means the virtual end of the particular union as an institution. A fifth factor, and perhaps the most important one, is the fact that the parties in many instances have not faced up to their real responsibilities. One might ponder about what the dimensions of the 1963 railroad dispute over firemen would have been if: (1) the companies had insisted on a no-hire policy when diesel engines were first introduced; or (2) they had not sold the nonuse of firemen on electric commuter trains for their use on diesels, because they believed the latter to be a minor invention as far as their impact on the railroads was concerned. The sixth factor, in the case of railroads, longshoring, and the building trades, is the fact that union organization has been by job rather than by firm or plant, making the change more difficult. This is because it has meant the end of the life of the union as an institution and because there has been little that could be traded for the lost jobs. In an industrial union situation many of the lost jobs in a particular craft can be absorbed in normal attrition and the union can trade moderate wage changes for all in return for the jobs of the threatened few. The essence of the whole affair has been that men of increasing years, relatively high past earnings, and few alternatives, are or feel that they are in danger of being displaced, and they resist.

In part, solutions can be obtained within the general context of collective bargaining. Seniority units can be widened, especially at the entry job level by making final layoff a function of company seniority and not departmental seniority. This would allow the burden of relative and absolute retrenchment to fall upon the not yet employed as was done at Kaiser Steel. Formal retraining programs can be set up with firms, and, in some cases, teaching skills required by other employers. This was done in the meat packing industry. Such policies are not necessarily easy to develop, especially in the heat of contract negotiations. A recent study of industry-union plans to cope with technological change suggests that the principal beneficiaries are those who remain employed. It is here, in efforts to devise, over a period of time jointly agreed-upon plans which can be "blessed" in some subsequent negotiation, that outside mediators and consultants may be able to play a useful role. If the parties to potential emergency disputes are making no progress and have not utilized consultants, a reasonable case can be made for *ad hoc* extra-legal assistance by the government.

In the main, the solutions appear to lie with the federal government. Some solutions are standard ones such as the general stimulation of the economy, increased training opportunities, and the facilitation of geographical mobility. In addition, there are suggestions of special governmental programs for the technologically unemployed. These might include extended and enlarged unemployment compensation, lump sum settlements, and retraining programs. See, for example, some of the recommendations of the Presidential Railroad Commission.

Suggested Readings

Irving Bernstein, *et al.* (eds.), *Emergency Disputes and National Policy*, New York: Harper & Row, 1955.

David B. McCalmont, "The Semi-Strike," *Industrial and Labor Relations Review*, XV, January, 1962, pp. 191–208.

Herbert R. Northrup and Richard L. Rowan, "State Seizure in Public Interest Dispute," *Journal of Business*, Vol. 36, April, 1963, pp. 210–227.

George P. Shultz, "The Massachusetts Choice of Procedures Approach," *Industrial and Labor Relations Review*, X, April, 1957, pp. 359–374.

CHAPTER 8

Employer Pressure

Employer pressure against unions can take a variety of forms. These pressures can be clearly illegal, as they are when active union members are discharged because they support the union, or the pressure can be clearly legal, such as taking a strike rather than agreeing to some portion of the union's contract demands. The more interesting aspects of employer pressure are those which may or may not be legal depending upon complicated circumstances, and those activities which have been viewed in divergent ways by various NLRB members and courts. Three of these types of pressure are considered in this chapter. One of these is the employer lockout. This occurs when the employer, after an impasse in bargaining has occurred, informs his workers that they can only continue to work if they agree to his position on the disputed point or points. If the workers do not agree, the employer refuses to allow them to work until they do agree. The second one is employer free speech. What can the employer say to his workers during a union organizing campaign? When can he say it? How must it be presented? Lastly, must the employer stay in business and deal with the union, or can he run away and operate with new employees in a new location?

THE LOCKOUT

It is the union which "hits the bricks." Because it is, there seems to be a layman's reaction which accords union policy the sole responsibility for the strike. Shortly after World War II, the United Auto Workers struck General Motors when their respective wage offers were but a cent or so apart. The question was asked, considering all the losses to the union member, why did the union strike for a penny? Few asked, why did General Motors accept a strike over a penny an hour in wages? A strike is a breakdown of a bilateral relationship, and it is impossible to assess blame without some standard of fairness and extensive knowledge of the specific situation. If, as the case should be, we recognize the ability of firms to precipitate strikes against themselves, is there any need to allow employers the right to overtly force the issue by engaging in a lockout of their employees? For many persons, the answer is a clear no.

A rationale for such a position might be as follows. It is the rare labor agreement which represents a net retrogression in terms of employment for the workers. The employer who wants a strike in the hope that it may break or seriously weaken the union needs only to offer no improvements until the workers either strike or the organization dies a slow death due to its inability to obtain any improvements. And, since such an employer is indifferent between a strike today and one next week or next year, the only employer desiring to use a lockout would be one who wished to harm the union or his workers by forcing them to take action before they wished to do so. Something like this analysis appears to have underlain the Board and court decisions which were made in the early days of the Wagner Act, for, though the basic statute contains no specific clause making lockouts either legal or illegal, the early decisions were adverse to the employer use of the lockout. This stemmed from the fact that many of the single employer lockouts were designed to frustrate the Section 7 rights of the employees and were as illegal as any other employer action designed with that in mind.

As is probably apparent, this defense of the no-lockout rule is subject to several objections. One is that, while some firms like shoe stores may be indifferent to the timing of a strike, many companies have strong fluctuations in their operations, such as the toy manufacturer before Christmas, the automobile manufacturer at model changeover time, or the drydock company with a ship about ready to go in. Slowly, as the number of relatively clear cases of coercive lockouts declined, the NLRB came to recognize the employer's legitimate business interest in the timing of a threatened work stoppage. In fact, the employer's justification of his lockout on the grounds that it was a defense against economic loss was carried to such an extreme (see *Betts Cadillac*[1] 1952) that one might conclude that any single employer lockout was legal, so long as the magic words "economic factors" as opposed to "bargaining advantage" were uttered.

A problem is also raised when an employer is a member of a multi-employer bargaining unit. If only one member of the association is struck, may the others lock out their employees? Boards prior to the Eisenhower Board would not allow the nonstruck members of a multiple employer unit to lock out their employees because the reason was concerned with bargaining strategy and not economic protection. They reasoned that a strike, actual or threatened, was a protected activity; therefore a strike of one member of the bargaining association was also a protected activity. Then the lockout of the other employees became a reprisal against protected activity, and consequently illegal. This doctrine was unacceptable to some of the circuit courts and three of them reversed the Board, though in *Buffalo Linen Supply*[2] (1957), heard by the Supreme Court, this doctrine had been upheld by the Second Circuit Court. In *Buffalo Linen* the High Court agreed with the Eisenhower Board that a lockout to preserve the integrity of a

---

[1] *Betts Cadillac*, 96 NLRB 268 (1951); 28 LRRM 1509.
[2] *NLRB* v. *Buffalo Linen Supply*, 353 U.S. 87 (1957); 39 LRRM 2603.

multi-employer bargaining unit was legal. The case did not distinguish the sources of the legality, whether it was merely an elaboration of the legitimate business interest doctrine which allowed defensive lockouts, or whether it was the beginning of recognition of a legitimate bargaining use of the lockout.

An additional criticism of a policy of not allowing lockouts is that it tends to preclude the employer from making major changes in the working conditions. The 1963 situation in the railroad industry is an apt illustration. Wages were sufficiently high and the change in work rules of great enough magnitude that a policy of "work, but no contract" could be followed for a number of years. Literally, the railroad workers were not without a contract since theirs has no termination date. The principle remains because bargaining over the rule changes involved seven years. The exact extent of the disadvantage to any employer is difficult to say, for he is free to change the conditions of employment upon reaching a bargaining impasse so long as he does not grant benefits which were not offered to the union during the negotiations. The only apparent danger is a determination that an impasse had, in fact, not been reached when the changes were put into practice or that certain demands were nonmandatory subjects and consequently not a basis for an impasse.

The future direction of lockout cases is difficult to predict, but a recent case illustrates a possible trend. A single food store member of a multi-employer bargaining unit was struck by the union. The company chose to continue operation and obtained temporary replacements. The other members of the association then locked out their employees and obtained replacements for them. When the new contract was signed, all replaced employees were taken back. The Kennedy Board took a dim view of this behavior and argued:

If the struck member operates through replacements, no economic necessity exists for the other members shutting down. If in these circumstances they resort to a lockout and hire replacements, it may be reasonably inferred that they do so not to protect the integrity of the employer unit, but for the purpose of inhibiting a lawful strike.

On the contrary, since the Respondents were continuing to operate and since no reason appears why they could not have continued with their own employees during a strike, this constitutes a temporary replacement of employees solely because they were engaging in protected concerted activity, i.e., striking against Food Jet.[3]

Neither argument is very sound, given that there are any legitimate defenses against strikes, though both would be consistent with a movement toward restricting the employer's right of replacement. Consider the Board's statement concerning the action "not protecting the integrity of the bargaining unit." The original rationale for protection of the integrity of the unit was that equal economic pressures could be maintained upon all members. Since, for the employer, operation with replacements is not apt to be equivalent to normal operation, preservation of the unit would seem to dictate exactly the actions taken by the employers in this case. Note, however, that the Board has implicitly assumed that operation with replacements is no different from normal operation.

The second quotation is even more curious. The NLRB held that the locked-out and replaced employees of all firms except the one against whom the strike had been called were discriminated against by virtue of their replacement. In other words, they were punished for engaging in protected concerted activity. And what was this protected activity? It was striking against another company. This leaves the Board in the position of saying that an employee cannot be replaced if he strikes another employer, but he can be if he strikes his own. Since the single action, a strike, minus other complications, can hardly lead to divergent consequences for those engaging in it, it would seem likely that the trend will be toward greater restrictions upon the employer's

---

[3] *NLRB* v. *John Brown et al.*, 137 NLRB 73 (1962) at 76 and 78; 50 LRRM 1046 at 1048: reversed 319 F. 2d (1963); 53 LRRM 2534; cert. granted 375 U.S. 962 (1964).

right to replace. It might also be noted that prior to *Buffalo Linen*, the position of the Board was that employees of nonstruck firms in multi-employer units were not on strike and thus protected. Now it seems they are on strike, but are still protected from replacement.

Policy on the lockout can evolve in several directions. If it follows what seems to be implicit in the just quoted view of the NLRB, it would mean that an employer's use of the lockout as a tactical weapon in the bargaining process would not be allowed and that the use of the lockout in multi-employer situations would be limited to the exact circumstances in *Buffalo Linen*. The rationale of preserving the multi-employer unit could be utilized to allow the multi-employer unit to engage in any form of lockout so long as it followed an initial union walkout against some members. The more revolutionary direction would be the recognition of the lockout as the counterpart to the strike, and minus an illegitimate motive on the part of the employer, a lawful bargaining weapon. A case in point would be the situation a few years ago in the automobile industry when the contracts expired early in the summer and the union worked on without a contract. The union waited until it was time to bring out the new model before exerting its pressure. Whether the automobile companies would have liked to use a lockout in June is unknown. It should be clear that the use of such a weapon in that situation would hardly have been coercive, though in 1935 or 1936, it probably would have been.

EMPLOYER SPEECH

Among actions forbidden to employers by the Wagner and Taft-Hartley Acts, none has as checkered a history, nor has raised as much employer opposition as has the question of the employer's right to speak freely.

While the exact bounds of coercive conduct are never easily defined, there has never been any doubt that comments like

"Wages will be 5 cents an hour higher if the union loses," or "If you vote for the union I will fire you" are illegal. But what if the words are "Unions are not in your [the employee's] best interest"? In the first blush and bloom of the Wagner Act, such statements would probably have been deemed unfair labor practices. The Board acted under the theory that the employer was required to maintain strict neutrality on the question of whether his employees chose to be organized or not. Its basis was that the economic power of the employer was such that any indication of his preference would tend to prevent the employees from exercising their free choice.

In 1939, following an investigation of the NLRB, the Smith Committee proposed a specific amendment guaranteeing the employer free speech. In 1941, in *Virginia Electric Power*,[4] the Supreme Court laid down the general rule that, while the employer was free to take any position he desired, vocally exerted pressure could no more be disregarded than any other type of pressure. The Court's position, while clear enough, gave little practical guidance to the NLRB in situations where the speeches were noncoercive, but were coupled with a few isolated acts which were unfair labor practices. Nor was such advice forthcoming, though the tendency of the circuit courts was to view the *Virginia Power* case as giving management greater freedom than it had previously enjoyed.

Meanwhile, back at the Board, a new approach to be known as the "captive audience" doctrine was emerging. Since many employer speeches were given on company time, the argument was advanced that compelling employees to listen to the speeches constituted an independent act of interference and coercion. The Second Circuit Court, while upholding the Board's order on other grounds, would only go so far as to require that the employer had to grant the unions equal time at company expense.

With the passage of the Taft-Hartley amendments, a section was added making clear the employer's right to speak so long as he neither promised nor threatened. The clause says no more than

[4] *NLRB* v. *Virginia Electric Power*, 314 U.S. 469 (1941); 9 LRRM 405.

what was in the *Virginia* decision six years earlier, and mentions no captive audiences. Nor does it provide a firm basis for determining whether something like "And the meek shall inherit the Earth" was a promise or a prediction. The legislative history of the clause, however, clearly seemed to indicate congressional dissatisfaction with previous Boards' treatment of employer free speech. The result was that Section 8(c) has been generally regarded as instructing the NLRB to find fewer cases of coercive speech and to give up the concept of a captive audience.

Four years later, in *Bonwit Teller, Inc.*,[5] the captive audience doctrine reappeared. In order to maintain output, firms are allowed to enforce no-solicitation rules against union activity during working periods. Because of the nature of a retail business, such firms are allowed to prohibit union solicitation of employees on the selling floor at all times. Bonwit Teller had such a broad no-solicitation rule and enforced it. Then a week before a representation election the company closed 30 minutes early in order that the president might make an anti-union speech to all of the assembled employees. A union request for a similar opportunity was denied. The election, which the union subsequently lost, was set aside on the grounds that the employees had been denied an equal opportunity to hear both sides. The specific decision is constrained by a number of qualifications, but in subsequent cases the Board did not allow these to get in its way.

Following the change in national administrations and a reconstituted Board came the demise of the new captive audience doctrine in *Peerless Plywood*[6] and *Livingston Shirt*[7] (1953). These cases held that an employer did not have to grant the union equal time, but that last-minute (24 hours or closer to an election) captive speeches would be grounds for reversed elections, though not for unfair labor practice charges. In the main, the courts have

[5] *Bonwit Teller, Inc.*, 96 NLRB 608 (1951); 28 LRRM 1547; enf. den. 197 F. 2d 640 (1952); 30 LRRM 2305; cert. den. 345 U.S. 905 (1953).
[6] *Peerless Plywood Co.*, 107 NLRB 427 (1953); 33 LRRM 1151.
[7] *Livingston Shirt Corp.*, 107 NLRB 400 (1953); 33 LRRM 1156.

accepted this rule. The guiding principle was set forth by the Supreme Court in *Avondale Mills*[8] (1958). It held that the key to the question of a union's right to utilize company property to engage in organizing campaigns was the question of whether the ability of labor organization to bring their message to the people was "truly diminished" by not being able to use the employer's property. The current NLRB, however, may be trying to revive the captive audience concept. In *May Department Stores*[9] (1962) the company had a broad but legal no-solicitation rule which it enforced against the union. Then the company on its time and property made a legal speech to its employees and refused the union's request for a similar opportunity. The Board decided that such actions violated the Act. To support this position, they read the Supreme Court decisions given above as support for the idea of equality of opportunity rather than the more limited one of making sure that the union had some access to the employees even if on less beneficial terms. The Sixth Circuit Court reversed, holding that the Board could not force the employer to make its store available to union organizers in the absence of alternative channels of communication not being open to the union. The Board did not appeal the decision to the Supreme Court, nor did it give up the idea, for in *Montgomery Ward*[10] it said: "Quite clearly, here more than in *May Department Stores*, Respondent's broad and unlawful no solicitation rule, coupled with its own use of company time and property to impress its anti-union propaganda on employees, created a glaring imbalance in organizational communication that justified the union's request to address employees under the same circumstances as had Respondent." That the company had an illegal no-solicitation rule is clear, since employees had been told not to discuss the union between 8:30 A.M. and 5:30 P.M., including lunch and coffee breaks, upon penalty

[8] *NLRB* v. *Avondale Mills*, 357 U.S. 357 (1958); 42 LRRM 2324.
[9] *May Department Stores* v. *NLRB*, 136 NLRB 797 (1962); 49 LRRM 1862: set aside 316 F. 2d 797 (1963); 53 LRRM 2172.
[10] *Montgomery Ward*, 145 NLRB 88 (1964); 55 LRRM 1063 at 1064.

of being fired. What isn't clear is why the employer's use of his time and property for anti-union propaganda is mentioned, unless the base for a new doctrine of captive audience is being laid.

The grant of the right to speak may be of little value if the content of the speech is circumscribed. In general, the liberalizing trend in the ability to speak has carried with it increased rights for the employer to make statements which approach the coercive. Comments like "unions and strikes go together and strikes mean lost jobs and sometimes closed plants . . . a vote for the union on Saturday is a vote for unemployment" have been held to be mere predictions of possible outcomes. In addition, in *National Furniture*[11] (1953) members of the Eisenhower Board held that the expression of a legal position does not warrant the setting aside of elections. In the specific case, the employer told the workers that their vote would be of no value since he did not agree that the unit chosen by the Board as appropriate was correct. He would therefore refuse to bargain, thus forcing an unfair labor practice charge which he promised to fight at least as far as the circuit courts. It should be noted that once an appropriate unit determination has been made by the Board, the only way an employer can get it reviewed by the courts is to refuse to bargain.

With the advent of a new administration and Board in the early 1960s, it was no longer possible for the employer to "predict" that: (1) if the union wins the election it will demand impossibly high increases in wages and improvements in working conditions; (2) the employer will be unable to meet the union's demands; (3) a strike will ensue; and (4) during the course of the strike the employer will either be forced to replace the employees or to close his doors.

In *Oak Manufacturing*[12] the NLRB held that statements like the above were a threat to go out of business if the union won the election, and they were therefore illegal. In *Dal-Tex Optical*[13] and

[11] *National Furniture*, 106 NLRB 1300 (1953); 33 LRRM 1004.
[12] *Oak Manufacturing Co.*, 141 NLRB 1323 (1963); 52 LRRM 1502.
[13] *Dal-Tex Optical Co.*, 137 NLRB 1782 (1962); 50 LRRM 1489.

other cases, the Board set aside elections because the employer stated that he would contest the appropriateness of the unit involved and thus the employees' vote for a union wouldn't be worth much.

If the Board is to follow a policy of not allowing predictions of the evil which will follow union certification, what standard should be utilized? Judge Learned Hand has suggested that "Words . . . in their aggregate take their purport from the setting in which they are used, of which the relation between the speaker and the hearer is most important. What to an outsider will be no more than the vigorous presentation of a conviction, to an employee may be the manifestation of a determination which it is not safe to thwart."[14] To some extent, such a rule could be brought into practice by allowing the trial examiners, who are in the community, to determine the context in which the words were heard. However, such a rule, while perhaps an improvement, is no real solution.

The problem may be seen more clearly if consideration is given to the other major area of employer discrimination—that directed toward specific individuals. In a situation where the employee has been told to cease his support of the union, the employee knows that the determined employer can find some grounds upon which to discharge him. Under the protection of the labor laws there is a reasonable chance that his unjustified discharge will be reversed. For speeches which constitute mass coercion, there are only two ways for the employer to enforce his wishes. One is to run away, e.g., to close the plant and resume operations elsewhere. The other is to shift downward his employment conditions within the constraints of the labor market. In other words, if the employer, for any number of reasons, has maintained employment conditions which rank with the very best in the area, conditions which exceed those which he would have to maintain in order to operate profitably, he could respond to unionization by making

[14] *NLRB* v. *Federbush*, 121 F. 2d 1954 (1941) at 957; 8 LRRM 531 at 533.

these conditions less desirable. The first response represents no problem, for such conduct would be a separate unfair labor practice. The second one does present a problem because, minus special circumstances, such actions would be impossible to document. It is these labor market constraints which would seem to lie behind the meaning of Archibald Cox's well-known quotation, "Words which may only antagonize a hard-bitten truck driver in Detroit may seriously intimidate a rural textile hand. . . ."[15] Labor market conditions in the first instance are such as to preclude the employer from lessening the net advantage of his jobs, a situation which clearly does not hold in a single employer labor surplus area.

Yet is ability to punish employees for selecting a union the only criteria? Probably not, willingness to punish is also required. Yet how is that measured? And what is done with a hypothetical employer who would only say, "I hate unions! I would detest having to deal with one! A snake is better company than a union man!" The import is clear that the employer would probably do what he could to make his employees' lives unhappy if a union were voted in. But is it illegal for an employer to tell employees the depth of his feelings about unions? What of being accurate? The general procedure, partly because to adequately police such areas would be impractical, has been to rely upon the ability and opportunity of the opposite side to rebut the inaccurate statements and the employees' intelligence in evaluating what they are told. Only in representation elections where the misstatements in question came too close to the election to be rebutted has any concern been shown.

For example, an election day disbursement of pay checks, $5.00 of which was in a separate envelope as an estimate of union dues which were only $4.00, was held to have been a material misrepresentation. The election was set aside. In *Haynes Stellite*[16] (1962)

---

[15] Archibald Cox, *Law and The National Labor Policy*, Institute of Industrial Relations, University of California, Los Angeles: 1960, p. 44.

[16] *Haynes Stellite Co.*, 136 NLRB 95 (1962); 49 LRRM 1711: reversed 310 F. 2d 844 (1963); 52 LRRM 2001.

an employer statement that "We are the sole source of supply at present for some of our customers. We have been told that we would not continue to be the sole source of supply if we became unionized due to the ever present possibility of a work stoppage due to strikes or walkouts," was the grounds upon which a new election was ordered. The Board noted that while the company talked of *customers*, only a single *customer* had informed them of his intention and the name of the customer was not mentioned in the report to the employees. The Board's action was overturned by the Sixth Circuit Court in a *per curiam* decision which said that the speech was lawful under the Act and the Constitution.

One of the more interesting of recent cases involved the *Exchange Parts Co.*[17] Here, before the election, but after the union had filed its petition, the employer sent a letter to the employees in which he: (1) told them that they did not need a union to obtain additional benefits; (2) asked them not to vote for the union; and (3) announced certain benefits concerning holidays, overtime pay, and vacations. The NLRB found that the benefits were designed to influence the outcome of the election and were, therefore, violations of the Act. The Fifth Court of Appeals denied enforcement since the benefits were unconditonally put into effect and were not conditioned upon a proper vote on the question of unionization. The Supreme Court upheld the Board, stating that the conferral of employee benefits while an election is pending does violate the Act. Their rationale was that, "The danger inherent in well-timed increases in benefits is the suggestion of a fist inside the velvet glove." The NLRB and Supreme Court position is certainly more consistent with other decisions than was that of the Circuit Court. Still, their positions raise some nagging questions about the fairness of not allowing employers to make positive as opposed to threatening bids for their employees' favorable vote. Is the following illegal?

---

[17] *NLRB* v. *Exchange Parts Co.*, 375 U.S. 405 (1964) at 409; 55 LRRM 2098 at 2100.

If you don't want your children in an integrated school;
If you don't want your wife or daughter in "mixed" meeting;
If you don't want the Textile Union's New York bosses to integrate
    you;
Vote against the TWUA every chance you get![18]

Until recently, while deplored by the Labor Board, such attacks
have been regarded as legal since the Act itself says nothing about
appeals to prejudice. A recent decision, *Sewell Manufacturing*,[19]
resulted in an election being set aside because the employer was
viewed as deliberately seeking to overstress and exacerbate racial
feeling by irrelevant and inflammatory language. The employer
circulated a picture of James Carey, President of the International
Union of Electrical Workers, dancing with a Negro woman, the
wife of a Nigerian official. Since only an election was involved,
the Board could do this since they are allowed broad powers to
determine the conditions under which these elections should be
conducted, and actions which would not sustain unfair labor practice charges may result in elections being set aside. Even stronger
grounds exist for reversing elections where the employer has appealed to racial feelings. The employer's appeal is partly to prejudice and partly to the implicit threat of having to work with
Negroes. Viewed in this context, a threat to force employees to
work with Negroes could be viewed as little different than a threat
to cut wages by 5 cents.

One last area is the helpful community. What can be done if
the local bank talks with those whose mortgages they hold, etc.?
If the hand of the employer can be found in all of this, he could
be held for an unfair labor practice. Prior to the passage of the
Taft-Hartley Act, the employer might have been adjudged guilty
of an unfair labor practice even if he wasn't directly involved, on
the grounds that the community was acting as his agent. The

[18] From Pucinski, p. 308.
[19] *Sewell Manufacturing Co.*, 138 NLRB 66 (1962); 50 LRRM 1532.
Second election declared void 140 NLRB 220 (1960); 51 LRRM 1611.

Taft-Hartley Act now requires the Board to use a more traditional legal definition for the word "agent." The election could be set aside on the grounds that the proper conditions for an election had been destroyed by the community activities, but there would be no way of preventing a recurrence. See *James Lees and Sons Co.*[20]

We may have dealt too long with this, for employers' concern for their rights and the concern of those who seek increased union organization have made it a tempest in the proverbial teapot. The key elements are employer opposition to unionization and labor market conditions. The first can be easily communicated even under the severest reading of the Taft-Hartley Act and the Constitution. The second, labor market conditions, is beyond the power of the Board to change. The limits of the Board's impact upon these conditions remain to be seen. A recent survey of NLRB rerun elections shows that of the 20,153 elections in fiscal 1960, 1961, and the first 9 months of 1962, objections were filed in only 9 percent of the cases. Only 17 percent of the objections were held to be meritorious (315 cases). In 212 rerun elections which had previously been marred by employer misconduct, the unions won 30 percent. For the 55 union misconduct cases, 36 pecent were won by management. Employer threats to eliminate benefits or not to deal with the union appear to be less effective than threats to close the plant, for 75 percent of cases involving the former but only 29 percent of the latter resulted in overturned results.[21] But after the election, what then? Consider, for example, a nonunion employer who has always granted one more holiday than the number given by the median firm in his locality. He becomes unionized and over a period of years as the median number of holidays goes up, his remains firmly fixed. Can the Labor Board find him guilty of an unfair labor practice on the grounds that he is punishing his employees for having joined the union?

[20] *James Lees and Sons Co.*, 130 NLRB 290 (1961); 47 LRRM 1285.
[21] Daniel H. Pollit, "NLRB Re-run Elections: A Study," *North Carolina Law Review* 47, Winter, 1963, pp. 209–224.

THE RUN–AWAY ISSUE

This section deals with employer removal of his business to avoid dealing with the union. This means that the action must take place after the union has appeared but prior to a first contract. Once a contract has been achieved, an employer who closed or moved his operation would be subject to a charge of failing to fulfill his duty to bargain if he didn't bargain over the terms and conditions of the change, or if the contract were still in force he could face a suit charging him with breaking his contract.

One of the more interesting policy questions deals with foreign flag shipping and United States unions. The question, well presented in *McCulloch* v. *Sociedad Nacional*[22] (1963), is the extent to which United States corporations can avoid American unions by registering their fleets in other countries. A similar question is raised in certain localities' subtle industrial advertising which implies that unions will be suppressed by the citizens of the locality. Here the question is the extent to which the employer, if he loses the battle to keep the lion of unionism outside his gates, can still win by tearing down the walls. This may be accomplished in several ways. The employer can: (1) close his plant in one locality and open in a different location; (2) subcontract a portion of his operation; or (3) close the doors and go out of business altogether. If the closed operation is sold and operated as an integrated unit by the purchaser, it is probable that the new owners will find that they have also inherited the union. The primary determinant would be the motives and attendant circumstances. For example, after engaging in unfair labor practices, a company sold an unprofitable branch operation to its former manager. The new owner was required to remedy some of the previous firm's unfair labor practices.

In the usual run-away situation, two principal determinations

[22] *McCulloch* v. *Sociedad Nacional de Marinos*, 372 U.S. 10 (1963); 52 LRRM 2425.

must be made. Is the new operation equivalent to the old or does it represent a new entity rising upon the ashes of the old? In *Mount Hope*,[23] a case mentioned earlier, a key point in the company's defense was that, while the original firm had finished both cotton and synthetic textiles, the new firm handled only synthetics. Of greater importance in deciding whether it is the same firm, its alter ego, or a completely new operation, is whether the actions represented a legitimate business decision or whether they were motivated by a desire to avoid the union or punish the employees for choosing the union. One firm closed its sandwich department and leased the machinery and space to another firm. It then contracted with the second firm to purchase the sandwiches. All of this took place shortly after the union had won an election there. The company defended its actions, saying it had considered such a move off and on for over a year and that the cost of sandwiches was 2 cents per dozen less under the new arrangement. The NLRB found a violation, but was reversed by the circuit court, which held in part that the Board could not disregard the testimony of the employer concerning the prior planning and economic justification because of its suspicion that he was lying.

The Board and the courts do recognize, to a degree, an economic rationale for going out of business. Does this mean that extra costs associated with having the union operation are a justification for ending an operation? It is clear that losses resulting from having had to meet a union scale would be grounds for closing even though onus toward the union was also involved. Whether these costs can be anticipated and the closing precede the imposition of the higher costs is not clear. It would seem to depend upon circumstances. One firm decided to close out an operation in about six months when certain fixed costs had to be incurred. A union was certified for employees engaged in that operation before the six months had passed and the company shut down. The Board found a violation, but the Sixth Circuit Court held that the firm

[23] *Mount Hope Finishing Co.*, 106 NLRB 480 (1953); 32 LRRM 1492; set aside F. 2d 365 (1954) 33 LRRM 2742.

did not have to wait for the newly certified union to raise costs, but since it had decided to close when the known extra costs in six months came due, it could accelerate the closing upon anticipation of the union induced increases. Yet, in a very recent case, *Star Baby Co.*[24] (1963), the NLRB held that the defense of not being able to meet the union scale was not a reasonable one when the employer had not even bargained with the union.

The best known of the run-aways is the case of *Darlington Mills.*[25] In April of 1956, the Textile Workers started to organize the mill in Darlington, South Carolina. During the period of organization the company warned employees that it would close if the union won. By May a majority of the employees had signed authorization cards, but the company insisted upon an election. On September 6, 1956, the election was held, the union winning by about six votes. On September 12, Roger Milliken, the president, recommended to the Board of Directors that the plant close. On November 24, material on hand having been processed, the mill gates closed. In the following month individual pieces of machinery were sold at auction. The company's defense or rationale for closing was that the mill was outdated, its earnings low, and its employees opposed to modernization. The case was complicated by Darlington's relationships with Deering-Milliken and Company which owned 41 percent of its stock. Deering-Milliken also controlled 19 other corporations which operated 26 textile mills, a research organization, etc. In addition, all final products of the subsidiary corporations were sold by Deering-Milliken.

When the Labor Board finally decided the case, it held that an employer did not have the right to go out of business because of an unwillingness to deal with unionized workers. In addition, it decided that Darlington was but one element of the larger corpo-

[24] *Star Baby Co.*, 140 NLRB 6781 (1963), 52 LRRM 1094.
[25] *Darlington Manufacturing Co.*, 139 NLRB 24 (1962) 51 LRRM 1278; reversed 325 F. 2d, 682 (1963); 54 LRRM 2499 cert. granted 377 U.S. 903 (1964).

ration, Deering-Milliken, and that both were responsible for re-imbursing the employees for their losses by providing back pay and new jobs. In this case the order meant back pay, jobs at Darlington if it ever reopened, jobs in the other mills of the larger corporation to the extent available, and preferential hiring for those for whom places were not available. The decision was made by a divided Board and reversed by a divided Fourth Circuit Court of Appeals. It has been appealed to the Supreme Court which has agreed to hear the case. The strongly-voiced position of the Board minority was that the employer is free to go out of business with-out penalty regardless of the reason. This view finds some support in circuit court cases, but there exists no clear-cut precedent. Nor is this surprising, for few firms are in a position to just close their doors, and those that are always seem to have talkative man-agements.

The argument for holding that Darlington and Deering-Milliken were one and the same firm was based primarily upon a compli-cated set of overlapping family and subsidiary firm ownerships which meant that Deering-Milliken could have controlled Darling-ton if it had so wished. This of itself would not have been enough to support the findings, for in addition to being able to control, an individual or firm must actually exercise supervision. The majority of the Board was convinced that supervision was actually exercised because of the number of services which were performed for the subsidiaries, including Darlington, by the parent organiza-tion. A determination like this raises some difficult points. For one, the legal status of corporations as separate entities should not be treated lightly. Nor should an administrative agency be too casual in deciding that joint ownership of similar enterprises means unified operation. Yet, a maze of conflicting corporations, perhaps erected for other legal reasons, should not be allowed to shield a responsible party.

Whether this particular decision will be upheld is difficult to say, for it is based primarily on the circumstantial evidence of continued capital investment, $400,000 in the nine months prior to the election, the pattern of interlocking ownership, the minimal loss to Deering-Milliken because the business could be and apparently was absorbed by the other mills, and the position achieved by management relative to the employees if the employer's conduct was not disallowed. In legal terms the case may be weak as evidenced by the fact that complete employee reinstatement at the other mills was not insisted upon.

In summary, it appears that the discontinuance of operations to avoid unions is not a viable employer alternative unless he is willing to abandon that phase of his business or unless economic conditions have caused him to give some consideration to his changed operations prior to the advent of the union.

When the Wagner Act was passed, the typical firm was outspokenly opposed to the concept of outside unionism. Therefore, the Act was designed to protect the individual against *any* statement or action by the employer which might impair his desire to belong to a union or to engage in union activities. This is still the main thrust of policy as it relates to employer activities which might adversely affect unionism. As such, the policy fails to recognize that the typical firm's view of unionism has changed significantly since 1935. Neither does it recognize that the strength of unions relative to firms has also been radically altered. How the policy can be reconciled to these changes and at the same time provide protection to those workers employed in contexts unchanged since 1935 is an unsolved but challenging problem.

Suggested Readings

BenJamin Aaron, "Employer Free Speech: The Search for a Policy," a chapter in Joseph Shister, *et. al.*, *Public Policy and Collective Bargaining*, New York: Harper & Row, 1962.

BERNARD D. MELTZER, "Single Employer and Multi-Employer Lock-outs under the Taft-Hartley Act," *University of Chicago Law Review*, 24, Fall, 1956, pp. 70–97.

DELL B. JOHANNESEN, "Case of the Runaway Mill: Darlington Manu-facturing Co." *Labor Law Journal*, 12 December, 1961, pp. 1189–1203.

CHAPTER 9

Union Pressure

_____

As the first draft of this was written in October 1963, the liner *S.S. America* lay at her berth in New York, her engines dead. The reason, at least the surface one, was a dispute between two unions, the seamen and the engine room officers. The seamen brought charges against the Second Engineer, claiming that he used abusive language. The seamen refused to sail unless the Engineer was removed. The company was willing to temporarily replace him while it conducted an investigation, but the Second Engineer's own union, the Marine Engineers' Beneficial Society, asserted that it would strike if the ship sailed without the officer in question. A company proposal to have the ship sail with the Engineer while the charge was investigated with the provision that if it were upheld a new engineer would be flown to the ship, was not acceptable to the seamen. The matter rested there. Complicating it was the long-standing inability of maritime unions to accommodate themselves to each other.

Farther north, Canadian-American relations became more strained over an inability to find a solution to yet another water-borne problem, the war on the Great Lakes. In 1962, Upper Great

Lakes Shipping Ltd. was unable to come to agreement with its union of ten years, the Seafarers International Union of Canada. Their dispute was handled under Canadian law which provides that the parties are freed of a bargaining obligation seven days after the report of a conciliation board. When the union and the company were unable to agree after utilizing the services of a conciliation officer and a conciliation board, the company, after allowing seven days to pass, entered into an agreement with the Canadian Maritime Union. This arrangement has been contested by extensive picketing of Upper Great Lakes ships by the Seafarers Union in both Canada and the United States. The picketing has been the subject of injunctions under state, federal, and Canadian law.

The reactions of many people, including some with a basic sympathy toward unions and their goals, is that unions do not have the right to strike or picket in situations like these, and if there isn't a law, there ought to be one. Yet, assuming the liner *America* was allowed to sail, what means would one use to differentiate between the seemingly obvious pettiness of that situation and the legitimate refusal of employees to continue under conditions which they and we would consider reasonably intolerable. Or if the interests of fellow union members in Canada are too far removed from those of United States workers, where is the line drawn, by plant, city, firm, industry, etc.?

The historical answer was the enumeration of a list of purposes for which it was illegal to strike. This doctrine of illegal purpose, first specifically put forth by Judge Shaw in *Commonwealth* v. *Hunt*[1] (1842), was destined to guide the control of union activities for almost 100 years. Then a combination of the stark bleakness of the American coal fields, the aftermath of the Stock Market crash, and the use of injunctions to prevent unions from inducing workers to break yellow-dog contracts resulted in the passage of the Norris-LaGuardia Act.

[1] *Commonwealth* v. *Hunt*, 4 Metcalf 111 (Mass., 1842).

INJUNCTIONS AND PICKETING

The Norris-LaGuardia Act prevented federal courts from issuing injunctions in cases involving labor disputes which were defined as, "any controversy concerning the terms or conditions of employment . . . regardless of whether or not the disputants stand in the proximate relation of employer and employee." If these words were interpreted in a liberal fashion, injunctions would be precluded in the situations cited at the beginning of the chapter. In general, courts have applied a liberal interpretation, though at times state and federal courts have tried to distinguish certain situations as when American seamen picketed foreign flag vessels operated by crews belonging to unions chartered in foreign countries.

The Supreme Court itself has engaged in some of this sleight of hand. Just after World War II (April 1946), the United Mine Workers walked out of the mines. Following a declaration of a national disaster by President Truman on May 4 and an unwillingness of either group to submit to arbitration, the President seized the mines on May 21 under authority of the wartime measure, the Smith-Connally Act. Agreement between the government and the miners followed, but the peace did not last. In November of that year the union was set to strike again over the administration's refusal to negotiate part of the agreement. Two days before the strike the government secured a temporary injunction but the miners walked out anyway. The injunction and a subsequent contempt holding were upheld by the Supreme Court on the grounds that Congress had not meant for the Norris-LaGuardia Act to apply when the federal government was the employer.

The Norris-LaGuardia Act removed a federal court's ability to issue injunctions in labor disputes. It did not legalize what had been illegal conduct, though this was to all intents and purposes the outcome. Despite the oft-voiced fears that the Taft-Hartley provision which increased the grounds for damage suits against unions would be the ruination of the labor movement, the reality is that money damage suits are impotent weapons to utilize against organized labor. Consequently, their number is and has been few. Thus, the employer's hope for legal protection against union activity lay with Congress and it did not act until 1947. Employers were, however, not completely without legal protection, for there were always the state courts, especially in those states where little Norris-LaGuardia Acts had not been enacted. But, experience there can best be understood after a consideration of the types of strikes and the characteristics of a picket line.

Strikes and Pickets

Primary strike.   This involves pressure by employees upon their own employer with the intent of changing his behavior toward them. Typically, its object is for higher wages and/or better working conditions. It may also involve a demand for recognition, a common situation prior to the Wagner Act, and is still found in industries like hospitals, which are not covered by current legislation.

Secondary boycott.   This involves pressure by striking or refusal to work on certain material against one's own employer or picketing an employer (not one's own) in order to force him to change his relationships with other firms or persons. When the picketing is directed against a firm for whom the pickets do not work, it is often referred to as stranger picketing. In each case, the object is to cause uncommitted employees, tradesmen, and customers to cease doing business with the offending firm.

What does one see when one comes upon a strike and views a man or a group of men standing or marching with signs stating that they have a grievance with an employer? At the simplest level, a picket is an informational device. As such, he is worthy of the usual constitutional protections for free speech. Yet, it is also more, for Gimbels is unaware that any specific person has read its advertisement and gone to Macy's instead; and the Liberal orator in London's favorite open-air meeting place at Hyde Park may never know that you went home and voted for the Conservatives. The picket, however, is quite aware of your failure if you persist in going through the line, and of your approval, or desire not to become involved, if you refuse. A picket line may have yet an additional dimension—an aura of violence. The scene of scabs on barges protected by armed agents of the Pinkerton Detective Agency moving silently down a river has happily joined the history books. But glass in the driveway and abusive language may still acccompany today's picket lines and the years which have passed since the words "peaceful picketing" implied a contradiction with reality are not so many in number. Thus, it may not be unreasonable to infer that even the single picket conveys something of physical coercion which denies passage, even where reason cries that justice lies with the other side of the controversy.

State Courts, Injunctions, and the Constitution

With these characteristics in mind, let us return to the question of a state's equity court jurisdiction. By the 1920s, most courts perceived a difference between picketing by a firm's own employees and that engaged in by individuals who were not direct employees —so-called stranger picketing. As the country moved into the depression years, a few of the more liberal courts took the position that all peaceful picketing was legal and that it was merely a form of communication. Then in *Senn* v. *Tile Layers' Protective Union*[2] (1937), Justice Brandeis, after noting that a state could allow stranger picketing, added a side comment concerning the free speech right of the union to make known its dispute with Senn. Whether this was meant to tie together picketing and free speech is unclear, though that implication has often been drawn. The case for their equivalence became much stronger three years later in *Thornhill* v. *Alabama*[3] (1940). Part of the legal code of the state of Alabama read in part:

[2] *Senn* v. *Tile Layers' Protective Union*, 301 U.S. 468 (1937).
[3] *Thornhill* v. *Alabama*, 310 U.S. 88 (1940); 6 LRRM 697.

"Any person or persons, who, without a just cause or legal excuse therefore go near to, or loiter about the premises or place of business . . . for the purpose . . . of influencing, or inducing other persons not to trade with, buy from, sell to, have business dealings with, or be employed by such persons . . . or who picket . . . for the purpose of . . . interfering with . . . any lawful business . . . shall be guilty of a misdemeanor . . ."

One Byron Thornhill, acting as a peaceful picket in an apparently uncomplicated primary labor dispute, was found guilty of violating this section. Justice Black, speaking for the Supreme Court, reversed the conviction in an opinion strongly laced with references to the rights of free speech.

Unfortunately, the world was not so simple and it was hard to intermingle the mechanisms of income distribution with constitutional protections. In the late 1940s, a union of door-to-door ice peddlers in Kansas City, many of whom drove their own trucks, tried to organize the rest of the local industry. When all the peddlers did not join, an effort to induce manufacturers and wholesale distributors of ice not to sell to the nonunion operators was made by the union. All but the Empire Storage and Ice Company agreed. As a result that firm lost close to 85 percent of its business. Had it gone along with the union request, it would have been subject to the state's antimonopoly law. To protect itself, Empire sought and secured an injunction against the peaceful picketing.

The case, when it reached the Supreme Court, posed a real problem. If peaceful picketing were only free speech, then the injunction would have to be removed, for, while conduct designed to induce or coerce another into the commission of a criminal act is not legal, mere speech directed to that end would be. In a unanimous decision the picketing was held to involve more than mere speech and the state court was upheld. Viewed narrowly, the case was unimportant, for, as Justice Holmes noted, there is no constitutional protection of the right to cry "Fire" in a crowded theater.

A similar observation would apply to several other cases, decided between *Thornhill* and *Empire Storage and Ice*,[4] where the free speech aspect of the picketing had been disallowed because of prior violence or because it took place far from the location of the actual dispute. The importance of the decision lay in its provision of a set of illegal purposes, for the thwarting of which, injunctions could be obtained. As time was to show, this provision was designed to grow and grow. In *Empire* it was a proper state law making an employer criminally liable for the action requested by the union. In *Hughes* v. *Superior Court*[5] the same protection was to be extended to enforcing the spirit of a policy statement contained in a state law, and, finally, in *International Brotherhood of Teamsters* v. *Hankee*[6] to upholding a common law right which existed by virtue of a state court decision. In the eyes of the court's minority these latter positions were those of complete surrender. Others saw it as merely the closing of a circle, except that in the process peaceful picketing had acquired a small degree of protection against the more arbitrary and all-encompassing efforts to restrict it. In other words, they interpreted the *Thornhill* case as a limitation upon the unfettered right of states to forbid any and all picketing and not as one making all peaceful picketing legal.

Meanwhile, in Congress, similar attempts were made to restrict the ability of the employees not to work by devising a set of illegal purposes. Most of these were introduced in the Taft-Hartley amendments of 1947 and some were elaborated and extended in 1959.

[4] *Empire Storage and Ice Co.* v. *Giboney*, 336 U.S. 490 (1949); 23 LRRM 2505.

[5] *Hughes* v. *Superior Court*, 339 U.S. 460 (1950); 26 LRRM 2072.

[6] *International Brotherhood of Teamsters* v. *Hankee and Demonstrators* v. *Union* v. *Cline*, 339 U.S. 470 (1950); 26 LRRM 2076.

THE REPLACEMENT OF STRIKERS

A primary strike, unencumbered by subsidiary activities and designed to accomplish the direct economic betterment of the strikers presents no policy problem and is of little interest. It has been and is quite legal, and it is unrestricted, save in instances of so-called national emergencies. There is, however, one issue which arises in connection with the simple primary strike. It is, what are the rights of the individuals on strike? Is a striker an employee? It would certainly seem so, and in fact the individual on the picket line considers himself as such. As an employee he is protected in the exercise of his rights as provided in Section 7 of the Act. Since one of these is concerted activity, it would appear that the employer could not rid himself of the strikers. Does this mean that an employer's use of replacements during a strike would be illegal and subject to injunction? No, for in addition to the employee's right to strike, the employer has a right to conduct his business. What happens then to the replacement when the strike is over? Basically the problem is one of weighing the impact upon the rights of the employer and the employees of a determination that replacement could only be temporary and limited to the period of the strike. The decision on this point came when the Supreme Court in *Mackay Radio and Telegraph Company*[7] (1938) held that replacements hired during a strike could be kept on after the walkout had been terminated, thus replacing the striking worker. All workers not replaced would have to be taken back and the replaced ones put on a preferential hiring list.

The above allowance of replacement does not apply in the case of unfair labor practice strikers, i.e., those whose walkout is triggered by actions of the employer which constitute an unfair labor practice. The protection of the individual's employment also ex-

[7] *NLRB* v. *Mackay Radio and Telegraph*, 340 U.S. 333 (1938); 1 LRRM 269.

tends to situations where an economic strike is converted into an unfair labor practice strike by the behavior of the employer after the strike begins. An example would be if the employer gave a wage increase to the replacement which was greater than he had offered the union. The worker can, however, lose this protection if he engages in violence or the destruction of property during the strike.

Replacements are generally difficult to obtain, which isn't surprising considering what may well be their length of tenure and the general social disapproval associated with being a scab. To counter this, can the employer offer them something extra in order to obtain their services? As has been noted, the employer is unable to grant them higher wages than those he had already offered to the union. In order to protect the new employees from layoffs once the strike is ended, the firm might consider offering increased seniority, though in the majority of instances where this tactic has been utilized, it was an after-the-fact gift and was properly held to have constituted an unfair labor practice because it punished those who had struck for having exercised their rights under the Act. Even where no illegal employer motive was involved, the Board and the Supreme Court have held that super-seniority violated the rights of strikers as provided in Section 7.[8] Realistically, this means that about all that can be offered is the promise of permanence of employment and a higher rated occupation than that to which they could normally aspire.

If an employer can get rid of his striking employees via replacement, what of the union? In 1938 the Board decided that, when representation elections were held while a valid economic strike was in progress, only the strikers would be allowed to vote. This is because a strike was considered to be merely an incident in an ongoing employment relationship. In 1941 valid replacements as well as the strikers were allowed to vote. Then in 1947, among the Taft-Hartley amendments was one which provided that a permanently replaced striker could not vote. This was somewhat

---

[8] *NLRB v. Erie Resistor Corp.*, 373 U.S. 221 (1963); 53 LRRM 2121.

of a contradiction in terms, for no definition of permanent replacement was included and in actual practice this is never known until the strike is settled, for conditions of strike settlement have included the discharge of all "permanent" replacements. The new rule also led to some odd situations. Consider the situation at O'Sullivan Rubber. In April 1956 the union won a representation election 343 to 2. An economic strike followed when agreement could not be reached on a contract. A year and one-half later when the work force consisted of 80 workers who had not joined or had given up the strike and 265 newly hired replacements, the union lost a representation election 288 to 5. Legislative direction again came to the fore and in 1959 an amendment allowing a replaced striker to vote in an election up to 12 months after his replacement was passed.

PICKETS AND MISCONDUCT

At times strikes are accompanied by general violence or violence along the picket line. For picket-line violence and mass picketing there is no real remedy for the employer save the police power of the locality. This may or may not be meaningfully available to him. The provisions of the Norris-LaGuardia Act preclude an employer's obtaining an injunction in the case of violence unless his hands are clean, which according to the Supreme Court means that he has offered to arbitrate the dispute. And, though the violence may well be an unfair labor practice because it amounts to union coercion of employees in the exercise of their right not to strike, the length of time required to obtain a Board order means that, as a practical matter, NLRB relief is not available to the employer. An employer could refuse to reinstate those responsible for the violence; surely he should not be required to take back an employee who has thrown eggs at his car or knocked down his fence. He would have this authority provided he had specific proof of their involvement and he would be required to treat all cases equally. The mere fact that the union apparently condones the action, because it takes no steps to try to prevent it, would not allow the employer to discharge its officers.

Since picketing contains elements of protected free speech, it might appear that speech used in conjunction with a labor dispute could not be the basis for discharge. This is almost always true, and the principal case *Local 1229 IBEW*[9] (1951) suggests how very special the circumstances must be for it not to be true. In this case the employees continued to work their regular shifts and engaged in picketing and publicity activities relating to their contract dispute only in their off-duty hours. Then for a period, their comments and signs were directed not at their working conditions, but at the quality of their employer's product. They were employed by a television station and the charge was that it carried mostly network tapes and gave scant attention to local material. The employer defended his discharges as stemming from employee disloyalty rather than from legitimate concerted activities. This argument was accepted by the Supreme Court.

The pureness of a primary dispute may be compromised if the union seeks to utilize slowdowns or work by the rule book campaigns or other forms of harassment to obtain their goals rather than an outright walkout. In the case of activities taking place during a contractual period, like wildcat strikes or strikes in violation of the contract, there is no recourse through the labor board or through the Norris-LaGuardia Act. To combat these the employer can make recourse to whatever traditional disciplinary measures he had used. He may also have grounds for a suit charging contract violation. If the workers take concerted action in violation of their contract to protest a serious employer unfair labor practice, the activities are protected and employer discipline would not be allowed.

For a brief period the Board attempted to police union harassment in lieu of a walkout. In one such case, following the expiration of their contract, some insurance agents followed a pattern of

[9] *Local 1229 Electrical Workers, I.B.E.W.*, 94 NLRB 1507 (1951); 28 LRRM 1215.

reporting for work, but they neither collected premiums nor attended meetings called by the company, etc.[10] The Board, after deciding that an impasse had not been reached, held that the union had failed to bargain in good faith because such conduct was not consistent with reasoned behavior. This was reversed by the Supreme Court which viewed the Board's actions as an attempt to control the conduct of collective bargaining in a manner not authorized by Congress. The opinion was a strong one and implied that under *no* conditions would harassment be an unfair labor practice, though several justices felt that certain harassment might be beyond the bounds, even though this was not true of the case at issue. In general, it would appear that the Court's view was sounder than the Board's. Once the campaign began, the firm could probably have locked out the employees using an economic factors justification or have taken disciplinary measures against the offending employees. And, it is difficult to imagine a situation where strikes are allowed in which the pressure upon the company of a partial strike would be greater than the pressure of a complete shutdown.

SECONDARY EFFECTS

Perhaps the most difficult problem, both in terms of specific solutions and in terms of the most desirable policy, is that of how much pressure from union activity an employer who is not the primary employer should be forced to bear.

It is clear that any primary strike may result in some business pressure upon secondary employers. In turn it is to be expected that these pressures will react back upon the primary employer encouraging him to settle the dispute. This influence seems quite appropriate and desirable. Indeed, it is unavoidable without eliminating the right to strike. In situations where the struck primary employer has continued his operations, the impact upon the secondary employer may be transmitted to the secondary em-

[10] *NLRB* v. *Insurance Agents*, 361 U.S. 477 (1960); 45 LRRM 2705.

ployer through the refusal of his employees to cross the primary picket line. Indeed, in the good old days when no self-respecting firm would have provided hot coffee to pickets, other workers' respect of the picket line was one of the few strengths of the then emerging labor movement. The secondary employer can, of course, order his employee to cross the picket line and fire him if he refuses, but he must take him back if he applies before a replacement is obtained. The union of the secondary employer could negotiate a contract protecting the right of the employees to refuse to cross the valid primary picket lines of other firms. They could not, however, negotiate a clause which allowed them not to work on struck goods for this would be an illegal hot cargo clause, a problem which we will discuss later. What should be clear, as has been emphasized by the Labor Board and courts, is that every refusal by the employees of a secondary employer to deal with the primary firm does not constitute a secondary boycott. If this is true, what does?

The basic case in this area is *Denver Building Trades*.[11] In September of 1947 Doose and Linter, a general contractor, awarded a subcontract to Gould and Preisner, a firm which for 20 years had employed nonunion labor. In November a representative of the Denver Building Trades Council told Gould he did not see how the job could continue with his nonunion men on it. In January of 1948 the Council placed a picket at the job site stating that the job was unfair. This was a signal for the union men to stay away from the job, which they did until Doose and Linter broke their contract with Gould and Preisner.

The union's defense was that they were engaged in a primary dispute with the general contractor in an effort to obtain an all union work force, an object quite legal under the Act. The position of the Board was that, since the general contractor could not grant the union's demand without terminating his business relationship with Gould and Preisner, it was a simple secondary

[11] *NLRB* v. *Denver Building and Construction Trades Council*, 341 U.S. 675 (1951); 28 LRRM 2108.

boycott, except that the event occurred at a common site. This view was upheld by the Supreme Court, though several dissenters felt that the decision ignored the reality of the situation: (1) the common site; and (2) the long-standing union tradition of not working with nonunion men. There is, of course, the other reality: (1) that subcontracting is typical of the industry; and (2) that certain public construction involves the separate granting of subcontracts which must go to the lowest responsible bidder, etc. Perhaps more important is the question as to what extent, minus specific legislative language, the apparent reality of the industrial work place can be substituted for the legal reality of separate corporations? There are times, of course, when courts will pierce the corporate veil in order to assure that a firm accepts responsibility for its actions, but it is not a common procedure. As might be supposed, this decision did not rest well with unions in the construction industry and they have made valiant attempts to obtain the right to engage in limited activities of this type from Congress. The policy has not been changed, however, despite the support of the last two administrations and even the approval at one point of the construction industry.

In addition to those in construction, two other common site problems have emerged. One is now known as the *reserved gate doctrine*. Industrial employers have typically set up separate gates by which employees of subcontractors engaged in renovation and new construction enter the plant area. Then, in the event of labor problems with either their own employees or those of the contractors, pickets could not be established at the other gate without running afoul of the secondary boycott provisions. This doctrine has been supported by the Supreme Court, but with the insistence that the work of the subcontractors be unrelated to the everyday activities of the firm; that is, the subcontractors could do their work without curtailing normal operations of the principal employer. In the case at bar, *Local 761, Electrical Workers, IUE*,[12]

---

[12] *Local 761 Electrical Workers, I.U.E.* v. NLRB, 366 U.S. 667 (1961); 48 LRRM 2210.

it was held that this condition was not met because the work being done affected machinery normally used by production workers, and thus the contractor's gate could be picketed.

If an auto dealer wishes to advertise by having radio broadcasts from his showroom, can striking employees of the radio station picket the showroom? In *Moore Dry Dock Co.*[13] (1950) where the issue involved the right of seamen to picket a ship which was in dry dock, the NLRB laid down certain rules in regard to pickets' use of a common situs. These were: (1) that the picket signs show clearly that the dispute is only with the primary employer; (2) that the primary employer must be engaged in his normal business at the site; (3) that the picketing is limited to times when the primary employees are present at the common site; and (4) that the picketing takes place reasonably close to the location of the dispute.

Later, in what came to be known as the "Washington Coca-Cola doctrine,"[14] an Eisenhower-appointed Board held that, even though picketing met the Moore standards, if the primary employer had a permanent location of business where the picketing could take place, then picketing could *only* take place at the permanent location. The reasoning by the Board might have run as follows. Since all the primary employees will go to the main office at least once a day, a picket line there can dissuade them from continuing to work. The same is true in terms of obtaining an impact upon the customers of the struck firm. Thus, the only value to the pickets from operation at the secondary site is obtaining support from the secondary employees or customers of the secondary employer, and this is exactly what the secondary boycott provisions were designed to prevent. In its purest form, Washington Coca-Cola was not approved by the courts and recent decisions have enacted sweeping changes in it, all in the spirit of Moore Dry Dock. The permanent location of the primary em-

---

[13] *Sailors' Union of the Pacific*, 92 NLRB 549 (1950); 27 LRRM 1108.
[14] *Washington Coca Cola Bottling Works, Inc.*, 107 NLRB 299 (1953); 33 LRRM 1132; affirmed 220 F. 2d 380 (1955); 35 LRRM 2776.

ployer is only one factor to be considered, though in *Brown Transport*[15] the NLRB found nothing wrong in a situation where for the first several weeks of the strike, pickets only appeared at the secondary site, a truck loading dock, and none bothered to picket the firm's office.

Before the Wagner Act, the recognition picket line was a favorite method of union organization. The Wagner solution of ordered elections, while removing the need for this tactic, did not provide any relief to the firm whose employees either did not wish to join or belonged to another union. Nor was such protection written into the Taft-Hartley amendments to the Wagner Act. Rather, it remained for the 1959 amendments to the Taft-Hartley Act to grant protection from recognitional picketing over an extended period. A proviso was added, however, to insure that nothing in the revised act prevented informational picketing. This has raised several problems of interpretation. Consider a union which establishes a recognitional picket line, applies for an election, and loses it. Clearly, the law now requires that the recognitional picket line be removed, and just as clearly it allows a "true" informational picket line to be set up. One question is whether, having started with a recognitional line, any "informational pickets" can sufficiently dissociate themselves, without the passage of time, from the original motive of the original picket line. The present Board's decisions tend to be that it can and their standard appears to be the words of the responsible union official. It is possible that the words on the picket signs would indicate that the true motive was still recognition and bargaining despite a disclaimer to the contrary. To date one of the biggest controversies has been over the use of "area standards" picket signs. (See the case of *Local 41 of the Hod Carriers*.[16]) If a firm is organized by one union, can another one picket it with signs such as: "This company not organized by ABC union and pays less than area rates"? A minor-

---

[15] *Truckdrivers & Helpers Local 728, Teamsters*, 144 NLRB 30 (1964); 54 LRRM 1093.

[16] *Local 41, Hod Carriers*, 133 NLRB 512 (1961); 48 LRRM 1667.

ity of the NLRB wished to treat such signs as inherently recognitional in character. What the final Supreme Court decision will be cannot be foreseen, though a strong presumption would be that the Board majority would be upheld and "area standards" allowed. One might wonder whether this is in accord with congressional desires, for there seemed to be strong sentiment in favor of stopping stranger picketing when the Landrum-Griffin Act was passed.

Much of American industry is highly vertically integrated. In this situation, the typical industrial union is little concerned about the employment conditions of supplier or customer firms, for working conditions over most of the productive processes are within its control. In industries like construction, apparel, and trucking where the majority of firms perform but a small portion of work embodied in the final product or service, unions have sought to enforce working conditions over the complete process by hot cargo clauses—provisions in their contracts that they will handle only union material or only material which is not associated with a labor dispute. A strong case for such contracts can be made upon the interests of the employees in protecting their hard-won standards. It is also true that these clauses, especially in a regulated industry like trucking, can be the vehicle by which union membership is forced upon employees who would prefer to remain unassociated. In fact, much of the success of James Hoffa and the Teamsters Union can be laid to his imaginative use of the principle of the hot cargo clause. Congress has chosen to give more weight to the principle of free choice in the choice of a union or no union as opposed to the principle of "common interest." The result has been outright prohibition of hot cargo clauses or anything like them, except for certain exceptions in the building and apparel trades in the Landrum-Griffin Act.

Over the years a number of distinctions have been drawn between allowable and unallowable union conduct. The earliest judicial proceedings would have disallowed all organized activities by employees. Since then, the dominant criteria for deciding upon allowable conduct have been: (1) what goal the pressure sought to achieve; (2) the type of pressure utilized; and (3) the relationship between those applying the pressure and the employer against whom it was directed. Primary peaceful picketing by a firm's own employees to obtain higher wages or better working conditions for themselves has, in most times and places, been considered acceptable. On the other hand, except for the period between 1932 and 1947, employee pressure against a firm other than their own employer has been considered illegal save for its informational content which has received constitutional protection since 1940.

Suggested Readings

Ralph and Estelle James, "Hoffa's Leverage Techniques in Bargaining," *Industrial Relations*, 3, October, 1963, pp. 73–93.

Donald H. Wallet, "The Weapons of Conflict: Picketing and Boycotts," a chapter in Joseph Shister, *et. al.*, *Public Policy and Collective Bargaining*, New York: Harper & Row, 1962.

CHAPTER 10

Individual Rights

___

No area of labor policy so typifies Charles Dudley Warner's adage that everyone talks about the weather but that no one does anything about it than does the area of individual rights. It was the right of the individual to contract for his own labor that was vigorously defended. Even when the exercise of that right resulted in children working for miserable wages under sweatshop conditions, it still rallied a Congress and a Court for many years. It was the individual's right to be a union member and still find employment which underlaid much of the concern of the Wagner Act. In both of these instances the milk of human kindness flowed only for certain individuals. The individuals were those who agreed with the policy of the time. Unfortunately, the world is little changed and true concern for the minority individual appears to be seriously lacking. The difficulties of the minority individual can be grouped into three classes. One deals with whether he must be a union member, another with whether he has an effective voice in his union if he chooses to be a member, and the last with whether he has any protection from collective action which affects his personal conditions of employment.

Prior to 1932, whether a person had to be, or could be, a union member depended entirely upon the particular situation, for it was determined by agreement among the parties themselves. In industries like construction, the closed shop was maintained, while in the coal fields it was the open shop and the yellow-dog contract. With the passage of the Norris-LaGuardia Act in 1932, it was no longer possible for the employer to enforce the conditions of a yellow-dog contract, though nothing prevented him from firing the offending workers. This liberalizing trend was greatly accelerated with the passage of the Wagner Act. Now the employer was also precluded from discrimination on the basis of union adherence and the closed shop received indirect support because the Act utilized the concept of an exclusive bargaining agent.

THE CLOSED SHOP

While the Wagner Act was being debated, the question of minority rights was raised, but a close reading of the testimony suggests that the chief concern was over the rights of minority labor organizations (mostly company unions) rather than over the rights of the individual minority worker. Little if any thought was devoted to the possibility that the closed shop might be operated in conjunction with a closed union, i.e., one which would not allow anyone who wished to become a member. Historically, this combination of closed shop and union has been variously viewed by the state courts. The more liberal view was well-expressed by Chief Judge Parker of New York in *National Protective Association* v. *Cumming*[1] in 1902. In a case where a union was striking to prevent certain individuals from being employed, he said:

. . . Their right to stop work is not cut off because the reason (which they give for the strike) seems inadequate or selfish to the employer or the society.

The usual state court cases did not involve, however, true closed

[1] *National Protective Association* v. *Cumming*, 170 N.Y. 315 (1902) at 321.

shop-closed union disputes. Rather, they were usually jurisdictional disputes between two unions over whose members should
do certain work. The seriousness of the closed shop-closed union
situation (one where employment required prior acceptance by a
union which would accept only individuals with special characteristics) between 1935 and 1947 has never been calculated. To a
postwar Republican Congress it appeared to have been serious
enough for it to vote to outlaw the closed shop. Even union shops
were constrained, for discharge for lack of membership was allowed only for nonpayment of dues when membership had been
open upon the same terms and conditions applicable to all other
employees. This meant that a worker expelled because he crossed
a picket line or who was denied membership because he was a
Negro could not be discharged. Since this is a rather simple requirement, one might be surprised if there were more than a few
cases involving this aspect.

Surprise or not, the Board has, on a number of occasions, had
to answer the question of at what point in the discharge process
the delinquent member must offer his dues if he is to retain his
job. In 1951 in *Chisholm-Ryder*,[2] the Truman Board held that,
once the union requested his discharge, it could insist that the
company follow through, even though the man offered to pay
what he owed prior to his actually being fired. Then in *Aluminum
Workers*[3] in 1955, the Board reversed itself and held that a valid
tender of dues prior to actual discharge prevented the union from
going ahead with its demand. Now, with the passage of the years
and the advent of a new Board, a new decision, *Acme Freight*,[4]
has been handed down. It has overruled *Aluminum Workers*
and returned to *Chisholm-Ryder* in holding that if the request for
discharge is a lawful one, then the union can insist that the discharge continue.

Three years before these Taft-Hartley amendments the closed

---

[2] *Chisholm-Ryder*, 94 NLRB 508 (1951); 28 LRRM 1062.
[3] *Aluminum Workers*, 112 NLRB 619 (1955); 36:1077.
[4] *Acme Fast Freight*, 134 NLRB 1131 (1961); 49 LRRM 1286.

shop and closed union were challenged in two interesting court tests. The Martinship Corporation operated a government shipyard in California under a contract which required it to practice nondiscrimination. As a consequence it employed more than 1000 Negroes. The union, not wishing to allow the Negroes membership but desirous of the dues, set up a special auxiliary local. This local had no voice in union affairs, but Negroes were required to belong to it and pay their dues in order to maintain their jobs. The California Supreme Court disallowed the arrangement by deciding that a closed shop and a closed union were incompatible objectives. The reasoning was based on analogy to public service concerns which are granted unique franchises and then must serve all equally.[5]

In that same year, 1944, the United States Supreme Court upheld a NLRB decision that the *Wallace Corporation*[6] had been guilty of unfair labor practices when it signed a closed-shop agreement with an AFL union which had just won a bitterly contested certification election. The basis for the decision was that the company knew that one result would be the denial of membership and subsequently of employment to the old CIO adherents. If the Taft-Hartley Act had not been passed in 1947, these two decisions might have become the base upon which a judicial theory of individual rights would have been erected. Too much faith cannot be placed in such an expectation, for in both cases there were unique circumstances. In *Martinship*, over 1000 individuals were involved, the distinction was based upon race, and the company operated the yard under a government order that forbade racial discrimination. In *Wallace* the firm had a prior record of favoritism for the AFL and opposition to the CIO. How different the outcomes would have been if the cases had involved clean hands upon the part of the corporations and had they involved only a few individuals, is difficult to say.

[5] *James* v. *Martinship Corporation*, 25 Cal. 2d 721 (1944); 15 LRRM 798.
[6] *NLRB* v. *Wallace Corp.*, 323 U.S. 248 (1944); 15 LRRM 697.

RIGHT-TO-WORK

In addition to putting a sharp limitation upon the ability of unions to demand the dismissal of employees for nonmembership, Congress in 1947 delegated the right to impose more stringent regulations concerning union membership to the states. This clause led 21 states at one time or another to pass so-called right-to-work laws or amendments to their constitutions. A few of these have since been revoked or modified. The history of that movement and the effect of these laws upon union membership and growth are largely beyond our interest. Suffice it to say that as a rule the more agricultural a state, the more apt it is to have such a law, and that there is little evidence that these laws have affected the growth of unions in a measurable way. In a few instances these laws have been the basis for state court injunctions against strikes on the rationale that an object of the strike is a union shop and hence the employer is being induced to violate a state law. The National Right to Work Committee and those who support such legislation insist that theirs is a fight for principle, that no man should have to pay to work. The fact that so many are unable to see the same principle when the applicant is black rather than nonunion, as well as other evidence, suggests that their position may well be less one of principle and more one of anti-unionism. This is not to deny anti-unionism as a legitimate position, but only to argue that it should not be hidden.

In part to avoid such laws as well as to accommodate themselves to legitimate minorities who refuse to join any organization save their church or to deal with managements which did not wish to force union membership upon long-service employees, unions developed the agency shop. This is an arrangement whereby membership is not required, but the payment of dues is required. As a device to avoid the right-to-work laws, it has not been successful. A recent Supreme Court decision held that under the law an agency shop can be banned by the states and that ban can be enforced by state courts.[7] With a few notable exceptions most state right-to-work laws cover this situation as well as the pure union shop. Left undecided by the Court, but with perhaps a hint that it would be decided differently, was the question of a true service charge. In other words, the union could charge non-members a fee to cover the cost of negotiating and maintaining the agreement. The size of the service fee relative to the regular dues presents an interesting problem and one that would seem to warrant discussion. The NLRB recently had a somewhat similar situation where they were asked to judge the size of the fee charged to nonunion members who utilized a nondiscriminatory union-operated hiring hall. In this case they allowed a charge slightly in excess of the union's dues.

The popularity of the true service fee may increase, not only because of the events described above, but also because of the possible outgrowth of a series of court cases, the principal one arising under the Railway Labor Act. In *Street* v. *International Association of Machinists*,[8] Street asserted that a portion of his union dues were being used to support political candidates whom he personally opposed. The Supreme Court decided in his favor, holding that he was entitled to withhold or have returned that portion of his dues which were devoted to the support of specific candidates. This result might be compared to *DeMille* v. *American Federation of Radio Artists*[9] decided by the California Supreme Court in 1944. There, dismissal from membership for failure to pay one dollar to be used to fight a referendum issue on the closed shop was held legitimate, for the political issue involved affected the institution's well-being.

[7] *Retail Clerks Local 1625* v. *Schermerhorn*, 375 U.S. 96 (1963); 54 LRRM 2612.

[8] *Street* v. *International Association of Machinists*, 376 U.S. 740 (1961); 48 LRRM 2345.

[9] *DeMille* v. *American Federation of Radio Artists*, 31 AC 137 (Cal. Sup. Ct., 1947); 21 LRRM 2111.

THE RIGHT TO MEMBERSHIP

As there are those who wish to avoid union membership, there are those to whom it is denied and who are desirous of enjoying it. These can be divided into two groups, those who object to their dismissal from membership, and those to whom membership is denied. Historically, the rationale affecting both groups has been the same. The courts viewed unions as private voluntary organizations with complete freedom to establish their rules of admission, conduct, and dismissal. This meant that about the only claim against a union's expulsion order which would be upheld by the courts was one that said the dismissal had not been in accord with union rules. Even this would be allowed only after the individual had exhausted all internal procedures regardless of the time required or even in the face of convincing evidence that it would be of no avail. In these respects union membership was treated in the same way as membership in a local church or sewing society. Since, when the Wagner and Taft-Hartley Acts were passed, no provisions were added to protect individuals, it is not surprising that the courts did not change their historical positions and move to a more vigorous defense of the individual.

Prior to passage of the Landrum-Griffin Act (Labor Management Reporting and Disclosure Act) in 1959, the individual faced two types of difficulties with union disciplinary processes. One was the criterion upon which a union could base its decision, and the other was due process. Though some difficult cases could be cited, the denial of due process appears to have been chiefly concentrated at the local level as opposed to that of the International Union. Once a case was appealed to the International, the worker was generally given adequate notice, the hearing was held before reasonably unbiased individuals, uniform penalties were levied, etc. In most cases final appeal was to the union's convention which meant that vindication or exhaustion of appeal could be a lengthy affair. The typical International also took a somewhat more tolerant view than the local of actions classed under the heading of conduct unbecoming a union member, which all too often meant political opposition. Even so, post-election vindication was a poor safeguard of democratic procedure. Legislation has changed most of this, for now the members' rights to vote, to nominate candidates, to speak out, and to be free of lengthy internal appeals are protected.

Does the new protection for intra-union political activity also protect the member from reprisal for his involvement in nonunion political activities? Many unions consider right-to-work legislation as a threat to the institution of unionism. In states where such a right-to-work proposal is on the ballot, unions generally mobilize workers, money, and members to try to defeat it. What of union members who give vigorous support to such a measure? Can they be expelled? Under federal law the answer is yes, for the union is considered the sole judge of its membership requirements. But state law may provide some relief. In *Mitchell* v. *International Association of Machinists* [10] (1961), a California court held that expulsion for vigorous support of a right-to-work proposal was not legal. The court stated that a union is unlike most voluntary groups because of the heterogeneity of its membership and the strong support it receives by virtue of federal legislation. In addition, the court noted that a member has an interest in membership beyond mere retention of his job, and that society has an interest in maintaining unfettered, the citizen's right to participate in political activity.

In addition to political problems there are also union rules which affect work standards or practices. Local 283 of the United Auto Workers[11] has for some 25 years maintained a ceiling on piece work earnings. Employees who earn in excess of the stated amount are subject to fines or expulsion. Expulsion would not

[10] *Mitchell* v. *International Association of Machinists*, 16 Cal. Rpt. 813 (1961); 49 LRRM 2116.
[11] *Local 283 United Auto Workers*, 145 NLRB 109 (1964); 55 LRRM 1085.

mean loss of employment, but a service fee would still have to be paid to the union by the worker and the worker would lose his voice in the determination of union policy. The Wisconsin Motor Corporation never accepted the arrangement and in negotiations tried to get the rule changed. As a practical matter, however, the company adapted certain of its practices to the rule's consequences. Several members of the union exceeded their quotas, were brought to trial before the union, and fined. They did not pay the fines and took their case to the NLRB on the grounds that the fines tended to restrain or coerce them in the exercise of their rights. In a split decision the Board held that union's enforcement of the rule did not constitute an unfair labor practice. The Board majority made this decision because the law clearly leaves the right to determine membership requirements to unions. The NLRB minority raised the question of why the majority's logic would not allow unions to adopt a bylaw prohibiting workers from filing unfair labor practice charges or other such clearly illegal practices.

The above argument by the minority is only partially valid, for congressional desire to protect a worker's access to the Board is clear, but its concern for earnings limits is unrecorded. A Board member's concurring opinion suggests that this union rule should be considered to be similar to contract clauses which grant top seniority for union officers, in the sense that both may work to the economic disadvantage of some workers. As a legal point this latter position appears clearly invalid, for the crux of the matter is the unilateralness of the union rule, for there is no question but that the company and the union could legally negotiate an earnings limit. Still, it does raise the question of why behavior which would be quite legal if done jointly should be illegal if accomplished only by the union.

Comparing this case with those providing protecting for political rights underscores a serious weakness in the Landrum-Griffin Act. To avail themselves of protection under the Landrum-Griffin Act individuals often have to go to court themselves and pay their own costs. For example, eight members of the painters union who were found guilty by an illegally operating union trial board, whose "unlawful" action was affirmed by the International, incurred attorneys' fees of $3475 in federal court action designed to undo the illegal act.[12]

National labor legislation has always made it very explicit that it did not extend to the question of who could join a union. If this seems strange considering the key role which government support has allowed the union to play, it should be recalled that unions were and are typically quite open in their membership. And if there is a single group disadvantaged by them, it has been the Negro. The fact that it has been the Negro has obvious implications for the difficulty of securing legislative protection of the right of open access to union membership. Not until the passage of the Civil Rights Bill did Congress see fit to act further. Even here, only the restrictions of race, color, religion, sex, and national origin are imposed upon union eligibility requirements. The "member" who is entitled to protection under the Landrum-Griffin Act is one who has fulfilled the requirements of membership. For example, in *Hughes* v. *Local 11 International Association of Bridge Workers*,[13] it was held that the law could be used to force one local union to accept the transfer of a member from another local of the same International. But in *Moynahan* v. *Pari-Mutuel Employees Guild*,[14] the court declared that the Act's protection didn't extend to an individual who had not received a two-thirds vote of the membership as was required by the union bylaws.

The principal legal challenge to the union's nonobligation to grant membership arose under the Railway Labor Act. A Negro fireman agrued that, under the Constitution, he had a right to union membership. The union, he went on to say, was favored by

[12] *Nelson* v. *Johnson*, 212 F. Supp. 233 (1963), 52 LRRM 2047.
[13] *Hughes* v. *Local 11 International Association of Bridge Workers*, 287 F. 2d 210 (1961); 48 LRRM 2734; cert. denied 368 U.S. 829 (1961).
[14] *Moynahan* v. *Pari-Mutuel Employees Guild*, 317 F. 2d 209 (1963); 53 LRRM 2154.

government legislation and thus was quasi-governmental, and thereby subject to the structure of the Fifth Amendment. The Sixth Circuit Court turned down this bid in *Oliphant* v. *Locomotive Firemen*.[15] The court's view was that enabling legislation did not extend the guarantees of the Constitution. The decision was no doubt a wise one, for the extension of constitutional protections to *all* organizations whose existence is aided by legislation exceeds the expectations of the authors of the Constitution, as well as those who sponsored the specific legislation.

THE PROTECTION OF WORKERS

If unions are not required to grant an effective voice in controlling their contract to specific workers, is there any protection for these workers? The individual worker has two kinds of protection against union actions which affect his terms of employment. One is that it is illegal for a union to cause an employer to discriminate against him because of his membership or lack of membership in any specific union. The second is the union's duty of fair representation of all employees within the bargaining unit. Can a union negotiate for employer contributions to a union-operated welfare plan? It can only if union membership is not a requirement for participation in the welfare plan. What if the union wished to negotiate a change in historic wage differentials between different sections of the work force, one of which was completely organized and the other of which had but a few members? The Louisville and Nashville Railroad employed both Negroes and whites as firemen, but only whites could become engineers. Until 1940, however, seniority for firemen did not depend upon race. Then the Brotherhood of Locomotive Firemen and Enginemen, which did not admit Negroes to membership,

---

[15] *Oliphant* v. *Locomotive Firemen*, 262 F. 2d 359 (1958); 43 LRRM 2159.

proposed that "promotable" (white) firemen be given preference
in layoffs and work assignments. In February of 1941 the company agreed. In April of that year, a Negro, Bester W. Steele, was
laid off and his job given to a "promotable" fireman with much
less seniority. Steele went to court and ultimately the Supreme
Court heard and decided the case. Chief Justice Stone speaking
for an unanimous court said: (1) that the union had a duty of
fair representation which required it to treat equally those whom
it was certified to represent; and (2) that distinctions based upon
race did not fulfill this requirement.[16] Similar decisions have been
made relative to the National Labor Relations Act.

The words, "duty of fair representation," have a ring of
strength, but, as analysis will indicate, their exact content is somewhat limited. This could be demonstrated by reference to different areas. Seniority arrangements will be used as an illustration.
Though policy, with the passage in 1959 of the Landrum-Griffin
Act, has taken an increased interest in the rights of individuals
within unions, it has chiefly followed the path of a concern for
the forms of democracy rather than one of an insistence that the
substantive result accord with the usual notions of law and equity.
Therefore, though present legislation may prevent a willful minority from denying a majority its rightful opportunity to participate, through its provisions for fair elections and its limitations
upon the use of trusteeships, it does nothing to insure that the
majority will not ride roughshod over the minority. Clearly, individual and minority rights in the work place may require additional legislation, though the politically realistic will realize that
the probability of imminent passage is quite slim. Some progress
might, however, be made under existing legislation via judicial
construction.

Consider, for example, the *Wheland Company*[17] which in

[16] *Steele* v. *Louisville and Nashville Railroad,* 323 U.S. 192 (1944); 15
LRRM 708.
[17] *NLRB* v. *Wheland,* 271 F. 2d 122 (1959); 45 LRRM 2061.

1956 merged two divisions into a single operating unit at the site of one of the former divisions. Were there any restrictions upon the right of the employer and/or the union to set the terms of relative seniority for the employees of the old divisions in the new operation? In general terms the answer is yes. They were subject to complete good faith and honesty of purpose in the exercise of their discretion. Specifically, the answer is no, except with regard to race. The rationale behind the perhaps warranted reluctance of administrative agencies and courts to indicate narrower limits than race to the meaning of "good faith and honesty of purpose" seems to be based upon the private nature of the contract, absence of specific legislative direction, and a belief that third party solutions tend to be inferior to those of the parties themselves. In an earlier period these may have been acceptable, but unions are no longer strictly private organizations. Still, as those who favor a hands-off policy would be quick to point out, circumstances will be so varied that a consistent policy setting limits upon the soundness of the parties' solutions would be difficult to formulate and apply. This is especially true because, while some violations of substantive justice occur when no individual needs to suffer any losses, the usual case involves situations where some losses of employment must be allocated among the various workers.

In one minor area of seniority problems, the NLRB does take an active role, and that is where there is a clear distinction based upon union membership. In the case of the International Operating Engineers Local 101, members of the parent local had more seniority than did members of the sublocals regardless of the years of service. In another case, a policy of making the seniority of employees transferred back to their old bargaining unit depend upon whether they had gone to and returned from another plant which was organized by the same union or whether it had been unorganized, was held to be illegal. Such instances of clear discrimination based upon union membership or its lack, are in the minds of some members of the NLRB, the only basis for finding a violation of the Act. To them, the legislation does not imply a duty of fair representation like that which the Supreme Court found in the Railway Labor Act. Illustrative of this is *Miranda Fuel*.[18]

Michael Lopuch was employed for eight years as a fuel truck driver for Miranda. As the eleventh man on a 21-man roster, he enjoyed year-round employment. On April 12, 1957, with his employer's permission, he left to spend the summer assisting his sister whose husband had recently died. He intended to return on October 15, but was delayed two weeks by illness which was attested to by a doctor and accepted by the company. Upon his return the union attempted to have him dropped to the bottom of the seniority list. They based their argument on the contract clause which designated April 15 to October 15 as slack season. This allowed men who would not have steady employment to take a leave of absence during that period without loss of seniority. If an employee returned after October 15, he lost his seniority. The initial demand of the union was based upon the lateness of Lopuch's return. After the doctor's report on Lopuch's illness was introduced, and because the contract allowed for medical delays, the union changed its position and argued that because Lopuch had left prior to April 15, he had lost his seniority. The company at last gave in to the union's demand. Lopuch then filed an unfair labor practice charge with the Board.

The initial NLRB decision was under the Mountain Pacific doctrine which made it an unfair labor practice for the employer to delegate to the union control over hiring practices and seniority. The Second Circuit Court of Appeals enforced the Board's decision upon this basis. The case was appealed to the Supreme Court which subsequent to the Appeals Court decision had in *Local 357 International Brotherhood of Teamsters* v. *NLRB*[19] overturned

---

[18] NLRB v. *Miranda Fuel*, 125 NLRB 454 (1959); 45 LRRM 1122; 284 F. 2d 861 (1960); 47 LRRM 2178; 366 U.S. 763 (1961); 48 LRRM 2277: 140 NLRB 181 (1960); 51 LRRM 1584; 326 F. 2d 172 (1963); 54 LRRM 2715.

[19] *Local 357 International Brotherhood of Teamsters* v. *NLRB*, 365 U.S. 667 (1961); 47 LRRM 2906.

the Board's Mountain Pacific doctrine. *Miranda* was then sent back to the NLRB which upon re-examination found (3–2) that there was still a union unfair labor practice. The majority held that it was an unfair labor practice for a union to induce an employer to treat an employee in an arbitrary and capricious manner. The two who voted for the union did not approve of the union's action. They merely felt that the law says nothing about arbitrary and capricious actions by unions that are unrelated to union membership. They felt that the union's action in causing Lopuch to lose his seniority would not come under the *Radio Officers*[20] case where it had been held that a course of conduct was illegal if it could be reasonably inferred that such conduct would impress upon individuals the necessity of being union members, for here there were no nonunion members to impress. They apparently didn't feel that impressing upon men the necessity of being *good* union members was equivalent. The Board was overruled (2–1) by the Appeals Court where the majority adopted the rationale of the Labor Board minority.

The difficulties posed by the duty of fair representation can be divided into two parts. One concerns those like the *Steele* and *Wheland* cases where the problem lies in the negotiation of the contract. The other covers those like *Miranda* where the contract is administered in an unfair manner. Solutions for the latter appear to be much simpler than those for the former. One solution to situations involving negotiations as described above is to allow some review of the substance of union contract decisions. In the specific area discussed, the allocation of seniority, courts would only need to conclude that certain aspects of contractual terms had become vested in the individual employee and could not be later bargained away by the union. One of the reasons, from my view, for the weak court positions on seniority has been that seniority has been held to be solely a creature of the contract and hence a union could bargain it away. This was the rationale

[20] *NLRB* v. *Radio Officers Union*, 347 U.S. 17 (1954); 33 LRRM 2906.

in *Hartley* v. *The Brotherhood*[21] where, in the face of layoffs resulting from the depression of the 1930s, the union wiped out the seniority of its married female members.

Does this mean that the union member cannot insist upon a specific course of action relative to his employment situation? On the whole, yes. If an employee has a grievance which he wishes pressed and the union will not take it, what then? The employee is free to press his own grievance but he has no power to either insist that the union or the company arbitrate the matter. Consider *Union News Co.* v. *Hildreth*,[22] where the company operated a lunch counter employing approximately 12 workers. Because of a rise in the ratio of food costs to sales, it became clear that food or money was being stolen. The company wanted to fire all the workers, but the union resisted and a compromise was struck. Half of the workers were laid off, and gross income then rose to $250 a week. Those on layoff were then discharged. Gladys Hildreth, a ten-year service employee, against whom nothing was proven, sought the support of the union in order to contest her discharge. Naturally the union refused since it had agreed to allow the company to fire whichever half of the workers included those who were stealing. She went to court, and those believing in innocence until proven guilty guessed incorrectly—she lost.

Further, should company and union decide to arbitrate divergent group claims, the union member has little recourse against the decision except if it can be shown that there was a denial of due process. In *Clark* v. *Hein-Werner*[23] the Wisconsin State Supreme Court held that the presentation of the claims of one group of employees as opposed to those of another without allowing the disadvantaged employees to be represented formally, even though their position was well presented by the company, was a denial

[21] *Hartley* v. *The Brotherhood of Railway & Steamship Clerks*, 283 Mich. 201 (1938), 2 (LRRM) 872.

[22] *Union News Co.* v. *Hildreth*, 295 F. 2d 658 (1961); 48 LRRM 3084.

[23] *Clark* v. *Hein-Werner*, 8 Wis. 2d 264 (1959); U.S. LRRM 2137.

of due process and illegal. This will not apparently be federal law, for under rather similar circumstances in *Humphrey* v. *Moore*,[24] the Supreme Court held that the failure to provide representation did not make the action unfair.

For many years individual freedom in the work place meant only the right to change employers. Sometimes even that was more illusory than real. Unions with the aid of governmental support, by their control over the employer, gave a new and vital meaning to individual freedom. The task ahead is to find ways to increase that freedom as it is threatened by the joint activities of these two institutions of the twentieth century, the corporation and the union.

SUGGESTED READINGS

ALFRED W. BLUMROSEN, "The Worker and Three Places of Unionism: Administrative and Judicial Control of the Worker-Union Relationship," *Michigan Law Review*, 61, June, 1963, pp. 1435–1528.

JOSEPH R. GRODIN, "Legal Regulation of Internal Union Affairs," a chapter in Joseph Shister, *et. al.*, *Public Policy and Collective Bargaining*, New York: Harper & Row, 1962.

JACK STIEBER, *et. al.*, *Democracy and Public Review*, Report of the Center for the Study of Democratic Institutions, 1960.

Summary of Operations 1963, Bureau of Labor-Management Reports, Washington: U.S. Department of Labor.

HARRY H. WELLINGTON, "The Constitution, The Labor Union, and Government Action," *Yale Law Journal*, 70, January, 1961, pp. 345–375.

[24] *Humphrey* v. *Moore*, 375 U.S. 335 (1964); 55 LRRM 2031.

CHAPTER 11

Some Final Thoughts

We have seen that federal labor policy is a complex mosaic composed of:

1. The specific words of the various Congresses which have passed the labor legislation.
2. The application of Congress's words by the staffs of the Regional Offices of the NLRB, the Office of the General Counsel, the Trial Examiners, and most important, by the General Counsel and the five members of the NLRB.
3. The review of Board decisions by the different Circuit Courts of Appeals and in turn, the review of their work by the Supreme Court.
4. The actions of the parties, unions, individuals, and companies, as they attempt to utilize or just avoid the application of the laws.

There are a number of different forces which have, and do, influence each of the mosaic's principal elements. For Congress, the evidence suggested that the tenor and tone of labor legislation has reflected the views of the party which controlled the specific sessions of Congress. This needs to be modified to allow for the profound influence of originally unrelated events which, when they have combined in certain years, have appeared to shape the dimensions of particular labor statutes. Though there have been a number of charges leveled against the NLRB, claiming that members were approaching the law in a politically partisan manner, grimly determined to overturn the decisions of earlier years, there seems to be little evidence that this is in fact what has happened. Even in a period like the early 1960s when the members of the Board were clearly split in their approach to certain issues, the vast majority of cases did not involve a dissent. There is, however, some basis for believing that the approaches of the various men who have been members of the Board have been sufficiently varied that the outcome of some marginal cases has depended upon the composition of the Board at the time they came up. Finally, the parties' own approaches to the law and the NLRB and courts have reflected economic, regional, and historical differences among the employing units.

A good deal of stress has been placed upon the vast complexity of federal labor policy, even in the limited area of laws governing union-management relationships. This complexity would only be broadened if other aspects of federal labor policy were also to be considered. A good example is provided by union-management negotiated private pension plans. Before World War II, few unionized workers were covered under private pensions, and if they were, the plan was most likely administered and controlled by the employer. Then in 1949 the Supreme Court refused to review the *Inland Steel Company*[1] case in which bargaining over pensions was declared a mandatory subject for bargaining. Later that same year, the Ford Motor Company and the Bethlehem Steel Company agreed to union requests for negotiated pensions and the pattern was established. By 1960 some 11 million workers or 60 percent of those covered by union contracts enjoyed some private pension benefits. The drive for negotiated pensions

[1] *NLRB* v. *Inland Steel*, 170 F. 2d 247 (1948); 22 LRRM 2506; cert. denied, 336 U.S. 960 (1949).

stemmed in part from the low level of benefits under the Social Security System. Had these benefit levels risen faster than they did, it is possible that the NLRB would never have been called upon to decide whether pensions were a required subject for bargaining.

There is, however, one aspect of labor policy which is both simple and consistently applied. Policy takes no account of the relative size or power of the union or the company, of their bargaining history, or of differences in the economics or structure of various industries. Such equality before the law has aspects like those noted by Anatole France when he said, "The law, in its majestic equality forbids the rich as well as the poor to sleep under bridges, to beg in the streets, and to steal bread."[2] To some people, this consistency is desirable, though a case can be made for the proposition that more complexity and recognition of diverging circumstances would better serve the public interest.

In what areas might it be fruitful for labor policy to take account of bargaining history, relative power, etc.? In discussing the lockout, it was noted that the traditional, historical, and seemingly current view of the NLRB is that any and all employer lockouts are illegal if their use is designed to obtain a bargaining advantage for the employer. This view may have been quite valid in the 1930s when an employer's ability to force a strike upon a weak union may have been the simple and easy way to deny Wagner Act rights to employees. Even today, most newly formed unions should probably be protected against lockouts. In the case of older and more established relationships, this proposition loses some of its force. Would automobile workers really be denied any of their rights if, after their contract had expired and an impasse in bargaining had been reached, General Motors was given the option of establishing a lockout rather than waiting for a strike at the time most favorable to the union, namely just as the new cars start to roll from the assembly lines?

[2] From Henry Davidoff (ed.), *The Pocket Book of Quotations*, New York: Pocket Books, 1942, p. 180.

Consider the *American Ship Building Company*[3] case. The company had been bargaining since 1952. In the years between 1952 and 1961 there had been five contracts, each one signed after the union had staged a strike against the company. In 1955 the workers had slowed down their work sufficiently so that a ship was caught in dry dock when the strike began. The ship was thereby lost to its owner during four weeks of his busy season. In 1961, however, the union officials assured the company that they did not plan to strike, even though they had conducted a strike vote which had given them overwhelming approval for a strike. On August 9, after all previous offers to the union had been rejected, the employer made a new contract proposal. The union rejected the offer, refused to discuss it with its membership, and offered no new counterproposal. The company, fearful that a strike would follow, closed down its operations and laid off its workers. The NLRB by a 3–2 vote found that the company's actions were a violation of the law. The basis for the decision was that the company did not face a serious strike threat since the union kept insisting that there would be no strike, and that, even if there was one, work would continue on any ship in dry dock. Regardless of the correctness of the Board's view of the seriousness of the strike threat, given the history of negotiations, were the employees denied any of their rights by the company's action?

The abuse of individual rights which took place in situations covered by closed-shop clauses probably justified congressional action to lessen the abuses. The congressional solution was to make any closed shop illegal. This did not take into account the extent to which, for a number of industries like construction and maritime, it acted as a substitute for the seniority provisions which are found in industries where the continuity of individual employment is much greater. The closed shop also served as the device by which available jobs in industries in which the unions had secured relatively high wages were preserved for those already

[3] *American Ship Building Co.*, 142 NLRB 1362 (1963); 53 LRRM 1245: enforced 331 F. 2d 839 (1964) 55 LRRM 2913.

attached to the industry and were rationed among potential entrants. In more stable industries, these latter functions are performed by a seniority system and the employer's hiring policies.
The union's ability to determine which new entrants will be
allowed to enjoy the high wages (a point of some contention
among civil rights advocates) may deserve to be eliminated but
is it necessarily less desirable than allowing the choice to be made
by the employer, or the allowance of the nepotism which accrues
with the inheritance of large sums of money, a family business,
or the provision of an expensive education? The point is that if
Congress had wished to prevent discrimination and to protect
the political rights of individuals, it could have done these
directly and need not have invalidated a contract clause which
served other useful functions in certain industries because of the
structure of their employment relationships.

As this is written the NLRB seems to be evolving a policy of
requiring firms which use their property and time for anti-union
speeches and activity to grant to the union a similar degree of
access to the employees. Leaving aside the merits of the approach,
it would appear that the important question is the extent to
which a union can bring its message to the workers without the
use of the employer's property. This will depend upon a number
of factors, such as size of the firm, size of the community, and
physical separation of employees while at work, but it would
appear to have only a slight relationship to the employer's efforts
to dissuade the employees from voting for the union.

Finally, in its recent *Tree Fruits*[4] decision, the Supreme Court
agreed with the Circuit Court of Appeals for the District of
Columbia that the NLRB had misread the law with regard to
consumer picketing. The applicable section of the Act states,
". . . Nothing contained in such paragraph (concerning union
activity against secondary employers) shall be construed to prohibit publicity, other than picketing, for the purpose of truth-

[4] NLRB v. *Fruit and Vegetable Packers and Warehousemen Local 760*, 377
U.S. 58 (1964); 55 LRRM 2961.

fully advising the public . . . as long as such publicity does not
have the effect of . . ." The NLRB read this to mean that *any*
picketing was illegal which was in front of a secondary employer
and directed to that employer's customers. In the case in question
the Teamsters union was engaged in a dispute with some fruit
packers. The pickets were posted in front of a large chain of
supermarkets. The picket signs stated that the dispute was with
the apple packers and requested that customers not purchase a
particular brand of apples. In order to make sure that their actions
did not prevent deliveries to the stores or cause store employees to
cease work, the pickets avoided the entrances to the store and
arrived and departed after the opening and before the closing
hours of the store. The decision that this activity was legal was
based upon the ruling that the only publicity pickets which
Congress had outlawed were those who: (1) urged customers not
to buy from the store because the store carried the offending items;
and/or (2) inflicted a harmful economic impact upon the neutral
secondary employer. The merits of the opinion aside, it could be
argued that since the probability of this type of picketing causing
serious damage to the secondary employer was small, it was in the
public interest to allow the picketing until actual harm was
proven. In the case of a large chain, like the one involved in *Tree
Fruits*, this may be true, but what of the small family-operated
and owned enterprises? Should they be subjected to the risk, no
matter how small?

The proposition that policy should be more responsive to
economic and historical differences among the parties has been
presented as desirable. If it were to be adopted, would it pass the
test of constitutionality? Could the law say that an employer could
engage in a lockout whose sole purpose was to strengthen his
bargaining position if he had had a bargaining relationship with a
union for at least five years or had signed at least three previous
contracts, but that such a lockout was illegal if used by any other
employer? A number of legal students would say no. Perhaps they
are correct. Certainly, in many areas of law, equality means treat-

ing all who engage in certain activities in exactly the same manner, regardless of their other characteristics. The traffic officer who takes a dim view of driving through a red light is not concerned with the size of the car, how long the driver has had a license, or, hopefully, how much he earns. This is sensible, for the goal of the legislation is to avoid accidents and facilitate the flow of traffic. However, when state and federal income taxes are paid, the magnitude of one's earnings does make a difference. And when many states pass Sunday closing laws, they exempt small family-owned and staffed enterprises. Thus, if these distinctions are allowable, perhaps similar ones in the field of labor policy would also be constitutional.

The basic aim of our labor legislation has been to create certain rights for unions, firms, and individuals. This can best be done when actions which can deny these rights are judged in the context in which they occur, for this may be the key to whether the rights were abridged. In addition, the legitimate desire of firms and unions to settle their own problems without the interference of government may be more easily accomplished if situations where there is a high probability of coercion can be separated from those where the probability is low. Lastly, it may even be possible to make the law more certain, for uncertainty is more apt to arise in a system in which deference to the context of the action cannot be given openly than it is in a system which openly considers the context.

PROBLEMS AND ALTERNATIVE SOLUTIONS

Unfair labor practice cases which go to the NLRB take close to a year to be resolved, and some take much longer. On October 8, 1962 the Kohler Company and the United Auto Workers signed an agreement which ended an 8½-year dispute which had included a lengthy violence-filled strike as well as Board and court decisions. Darlington Mills' reaction to a Labor Board election in September, 1956 is only pending before the Supreme Court in

August, 1964. The contract negotiations between the General Electric Company and the International Union of Electrical Workers in 1960 resulted in the union bringing charges against the company of a failure to bargain in good faith. The trial examiner's report was not issued until April, 1963 and in August, 1964 it still awaits a Board decision, and in all probability circuit court and Supreme Court determinations as well.

Long delays like these give rise to several questions. How effective is the law against an employer who is determined to avoid or defeat the union? In other words, faced with an adamant anti-union employer, is the average worker confident enough that his rights will be protected that he will utilize them if the best he is offered is that he will probably receive back pay with interest a year or so later? If the answer is no, one solution would be to instruct the General Counsel to use preventive injunctions. This would mean that if the General Counsel felt that a worker had been wrongfully discharged, he would secure an injunction which would require the employer to continue to employ the individual during the period of the legal proceedings. Since the General Counsel wins more than 70 percent of his cases, the impact would not be revolutionary, especially if it were only used in cases in which the legal basis for the complaint was already quite clear. The Act already gives the Board the right to apply for discretionary injunctive relief in any case in which the General Counsel has issued a complaint. This right has been infrequently used. From 1947 through 1960 only 48 applications for such injunctions were made and between June, 1961 and July, 1962 an additional 14 were requested. While the NLRB has the authority to adopt a policy of preventive injunctions, this was not the intent of Congress when it wrote that section of the law; consequently, such a policy should be established by specific legislation.

The current case load of the NLRB is 14,000 unfair labor practice cases, which represents nearly a 100 percent increase since 1958. This case load reflects several factors. One is the extent to which a number of firms and unions have not accepted the principles of the Wagner and Taft-Hartley Acts. A second is that many of the parties appear either not to know what the law requires of them, or to forget it in the heat of the moment. A third is that our laws prescribe the conditions of the employment relationship in greater detail than is true of other countries. In part, the latter is a characteristic of life in the United States. Even manuscripts and records from the Colonial period indicate that we are a litigious people and there is a strong tendency to follow up, "There ought to be a law," with a law.

If it seems desirable to reduce the case load, there are two alternatives. If unions and employers are using the law for their own ends, this could be prevented by reducing the Act's degree of regulation or by adopting some other measure which would remove the profit from using the procedures of the Act to gain a bargaining advantage. Alternatively, if more were known about the degree to which Board and court determinations really affect the economics of the employment relationship, the Act could be pruned of those sections which appear to have but a slight impact. Knowledge of the law's actual role in affecting employment relationships would require considerable research. The data cited in earlier chapters provide some insights, but they do not go far enough. One-third of rerun elections may result in the opposite group winning the second time and over 80 percent of duty to bargain cases may end with contracts signed, but these data do not provide a clear indication of the kinds of differences which have actually occurred in the employment relationship. Are wages higher, workers happier, etc.? Nor do we have any idea of the number of model unions and firms which would act differently if current legislation were altered.

Among suggested additions to federal labor statutes, probably none has as venerable a record as the proposal to place unions under the anti-trust laws. Like many policy proposals, especially the more emotional ones, the proposal's specific provisions are seldom developed. The proposal has three possible aspects. Many proponents of an anti-trust law for unions seem to feel that unions should have their ability to obtain wage increases reduced. This could be done by making it a violation of the anti-trust law for any group to combine to obtain higher wages. This would make all union activity illegal. A second possibility would be to return to the situation in the period of the 1920s when unions were covered by the anti-trust laws. This would present two difficulties. Large international unions engaged in pattern bargaining with all of the principal producers of an industry did not exist in the 1920s. Consequently, there are no clear precedents by which to judge what type of behavior would be legal and what type illegal. Further, as reference to the court cases of the 1920s makes clear, the principal behavior which the anti-trust laws curbed was the use of secondary boycotts. Since this is now accomplished by the Taft-Hartley and Landrum-Griffin Acts, the inclusion of unions in anti-trust laws is unnecessary. Or, in other words, at least as historically applied, unions are already subject to the anti-trust laws. One can also view the demand in what would seem to be its proper focus, as having little if anything to do with anti-trust, but rather as a proposal that the economic power of some unions should be reduced. Viewed in this way, objective and sensible policy measures to obtain this goal could be worked out. The characteristics of such a measure are closely tied up to the determinants of union and industrial economic power and that takes us away from the content of this short book. More research will be necessary, for few who propose an anti-trust solution appear to have considered how it would deal with construction unions or whether, for example, separate unions in an auto industry composed of two major firms would make any difference in that industry's wage levels.

Senator Everett Dirksen has called the regulatory agencies, of which the NLRB is one, ". . . The headless fourth branch of government." In this role these agencies perform some of the functions of the traditional three branches of government. In the case of the NLRB, its most prominent function is its adjudication of unfair labor practices, which is similar to the role played by the judicial branch in many other areas of policy. This has resulted in the suggestion that the NLRB's jurisdiction over unfair labor practice cases be transferred to the federal district courts. The usual rationale is that this will make unfair labor practice proceedings more courtlike and less subject to the political changes which may affect the Board because of the member's short five-year term of office. The impact upon labor relations of a transfer of jurisdiction is difficult to predict without knowing the complete conditions of the transfer. If, for example, the transfer only meant that the Office of the General Counsel presented complaint cases before a judge rather than a trial examiner, the impact upon present policy would be much less than if labor cases had to vie with all of the other types of cases which are the business of the federal attorneys' offices. The impact would also depend upon the degree to which Supreme Court decisions would influence district court judges, for even a casual examination of Supreme Court cases will indicate that Board decisions favorable to unions have usually been well received and that the Supreme Court has tended to agree more often with the Board than it has with the Circuit Courts of Appeals. The proposal to transfer jurisdiction is also somewhat suspect, because those who make it are usually unhappy over the trend of certain decisions, and they would appear to be more honest if they were to seek specific statutory changes rather than such an indirect one. And, if the only problem is that the current system is not enough like a court, the simple solution would seem to be to lengthen the term of office for NLRB members and increase their salary and that of the trial examiners.

Neither the suggestion that unions be brought under the anti-trust laws, nor the suggestion that the jurisdiction of the NLRB over unfair labor practices be delegated to the federal district courts appear to be desirable ones. The weakness in these proposals stems from a failure to correctly relate policy instruments to policy goals. Those who support these measures appear to seek a reduction in the power and influence of labor unions. If such a reduction is necessary or wise, then the measures for accomplishing it should be designed for the specific problem, rather than be imperfect ones with an aura of fairness.

THE FUTURE

Federal labor policy has passed through a number of stages. The Wagner Act was in response to the real need of the individual worker who wished to join a union to be free of abuse from his employer. The growth of unions, spurred by the Wagner Act and the wartime Labor Boards resulted in an enlargement of certain undesirable activities by unions and these required legislation like that provided in the Taft-Hartley Act. The Landrum-Griffin Act and the labor title to the Civil Rights Act of 1964 were necessary to make sure that organized labor, which was encouraged in order to bring elements of dignity to the worker in his employment, would not deny that same dignity to particular individuals or minority groups. In addition, each of these Acts bears the imprint of a series of external events that occurred in the period in which they were enacted.

If anything is clear in a crystal ball, it is that future years will bring new sets of difficulties which are associated with the employment relationship. These may well lead to the passage of additional legislation. The direction which new legislation will take is difficult to predict. If teaching, medical service occupations, state and local government, along with other sections of non-manufacturing continue to be the areas of expanding employment, and if many employees in these areas are denied rights which would be theirs, were they subject to federal labor policy, then legislation extending collective bargaining rights to them may well be forthcoming. Alternatively, if the power of entrenched unionism in areas of declining employment should lead to a serious distortion in the industrial distribution of wages, then at the same time that unions would be encouraged in service industries, increased restrictions may be placed upon the economic power of existing unionism. But regardless of the specifics, it can be confidently predicted that the area of federal labor policy will continue to be one of fascination as it evolves in a varied pattern, often expected, yet sometimes surprising.

Suggested Reading

Douglass V. Brown, "The Impact of Some NLRB Decisions," *Proceedings, Industrial Relations Research Association*, May, 1961.

APPENDIXES

Excerpts from the
Norris-LaGuardia Act[1]

SECTION 4. No court of the United States shall have jurisdiction to issue any restraining order or temporary or permanent injunction in any case involving or growing out of any labor dispute to prohibit any person or persons participating or interested in such dispute (as these terms are herein defined) from doing, whether singly or in concert, any of the following acts:

(a) Ceasing or refusing to perform any work or to remain in any relation of employment;

(b) Becoming or remaining a member of any labor organization or of any employer organization, regardless of any such undertaking or promise as is described in Section 3 of this Act;

(c) Paying or giving to, or withholding from, any person participating or interested in such labor dispute, any strike or unemployment benefits or insurance, or other moneys or things of value;

(d) By all lawful means aiding any person participating or interested in any labor dispute who is being proceeded against in, or is prosecuting, any action or suit in any court of the United States or of any State;

(e) Giving publicity to the existence of, or the facts involved in, any labor dispute, whether by advertising, speaking, pa-

[1] March 23, 1932, C. 90, Secs. 4 and 13, 47 Stat. 70 and 73.

trolling, or by any other method not involving fraud or violence;

(f) Assembling peaceably to act or to organize to act in promotion of their interests in a labor dispute;

(g) Advising or notifying any person of an intention to do any of the acts heretofore specified;

(h) Agreeing with other persons to do or not to do any of the acts heretofore specified; and

(i) Advising, urging, or otherwise causing or inducing without fraud or violence the acts heretofore specified, regardless of any such undertaking or promise as is described in Section 3 of this Act.

SECTION 13.   When used in this Act, and for the purposes of this Act—

(a) A case shall be held to involve or to grow out of a labor dispute when the case involves persons who are engaged in the same industry, trade, craft, or occupation; or have direct or indirect interests therein; or who are employees of the same employer; or who are members of the same or an affiliated organization of employers or employees; whether such dispute is (1) between one or more employers or associations of employers and one or more employees or associations of employees; (2) between one or more employers or associations of employers and one or more employers or associations of employers; or (3) between one or more employees or associations of employees and one or more employees or associations of employees; or when the case involves any conflicting or competing interests in a "labor dispute" (as hereinafter defined) of "persons participating or interested" therein (as hereinafter defined).

(b) A person or association shall be held to be a person participating or interested in a labor dispute if relief is sought against him or it, and if he or it is engaged in the same industry, trade, craft, or occupation in which such dispute occurs, or has a direct or indirect interest therein, or is a member, officer, or agent of any association composed in whole or in part of employers or employees engaged in such industry, trade, craft, or occupation.

(c) The term "labor dispute" includes any controversy concerning terms or conditions of employment, or concerning the association or representation of persons in negotiating, fixing, maintaining, changing, or seeking to arrange terms or conditions of employment, regardless of whether or not the disputants stand in the proximate relation of employer and employee.

Sections 7 and 8 of the National Labor Relations Act[1]

NOTE: In the material below, words in roman type are from the Wagner Act, words in *italic type* were added by the Taft-Hartley Act; words in ***boldface italic type*** were added by the Landrum-Griffin Act; and the words in [brackets] were added by Taft-Hartley and taken out by Landrum-Griffin.

SECTION 7. Employees shall have the right to self-organization, to form, join, or assist labor organizations, to bargain collectively through representatives of their own choosing, and to engage in *other* concerted activities for the purpose of collective bargaining or other mutual aid or protection, *and shall also have the right to refrain from any or all of such activities except to the extent that such right may be affected by an agreement requiring membership in a labor organization as a condition of employment as authorized in Section 8 (a) (3).*

SECTION 8 (*a*) It shall be an unfair labor practice for an employer—

    (1) to interfere with, restrain, or coerce employees in the exercise of the rights guaranteed in Section 7;

    (2) to dominate or interfere with the formation or administration of any labor organization or contribute financial or other support to it: Provided, That subject to rules and regulations made and published by the Board pursuant to section 6, an

[1] (Wagner Act), July 5, 1935, C. 372, 49 Stat. 452, as amended by Title I of the Labor Management Relations Act of 1947 (Taft-Hartley Act), June 23, 1947, C. 120, Title I, 61 Stat. 140 and as further amended by Title VII of the Labor-Management Reporting and Disclosure Act of 1959 (Landrum-Griffin Act), September 14, 1959, Public Law 86-257, 73 Stat. 519.

employer shall not be prohibited from permitting employees to confer with him during working hours without loss of time or pay;

(3) by discrimination in regard to hire or tenure of employment or any term or condition of employment to encourage or discourage membership in any labor organization: Provided, That nothing in this Act, or in any other statute of the United States, shall preclude an employer from making an agreement with a labor organization (not established, maintained, or assisted by any action defined in Section 8 (a) of this Act as an unfair labor practice) to require as a condition of employment membership therein *on or after the thirtieth day following the beginning of such employment or the effective date of such agreement, whichever is the later,* (i) if such labor organization is the representative of the employees as provided in Section 9 (a), in the appropriate collective-bargaining unit covered by such agreement when made . . . *and* (ii) *unless following an election held as provided in Section 9 (e) within one year preceding the effective date of such agreement, the Board shall have certified that at least a majority of the employees eligible to vote in such election have voted to rescind the authority of such labor organization to make such an agreement: Provided further, That no employer shall justify any discrimination against an employee for non-membership in a labor organization* (A) *if he has reasonable grounds for believing that such membership was not available to the employee on the same terms and conditions generally applicable to other members, or* (B) *if he has reasonable grounds for believing that membership was denied or terminated for reasons other than the failure of the employee to tender the periodic dues and the initiation fees uniformly required as a condition of acquiring or retaining membership;*

(4) to discharge or otherwise discriminate against an employee because he has filed charges or given testimony under this Act;

(5) to refuse to bargain collectively with the representatives of his employees, subject to the provisions of Section 9 (a).

(b) *It shall be an unfair labor practice for a labor organization or its agents—*

(1) *to restrain or coerce* (A) *employees in the exercise of the rights guaranteed in Section 7: Provided, That this paragraph shall not impair the right of a labor organization to prescribe its own rules with respect to the acquisition or retention of membership therein; or* (B) *an employer in the selection of his representatives for the purposes of collective bargaining or the adjustment of grievances;*

(2) *to cause or attempt to cause an employer to discriminate against an employee in violation of subsection* (a) (3) *or to discriminate against an employee with respect to whom membership in such organization has been denied or terminated on some ground other than his failure to tender the periodic dues and the initiation fees uniformly required as a condition of acquiring or retaining membership;*

(3) *to refuse to bargain collectively with an employer, provided it is the representative of his employees subject to the provisions of Section 9* (a);

(4) (i)*to engage in, or to induce or encourage* [the employees of any employer] **any individual employed by any person engaged in commerce or in an industry affecting commerce** to engage in, a strike or a [concerted] *refusal in the course of* [their] **his** *employment to use, manufacture, process, transport, or otherwise handle or work on any goods, articles, materials, or commodities or to perform any services* [,] **; or (ii) to threaten, coerce, or restrain any person engaged in commerce or in an industry affecting commerce, where in either case an object thereof is:**

(A) *forcing or requiring any employer or self-employed person to join any labor or employer organization or* [any employer or other person to cease using, selling, handling, transporting, or otherwise dealing in the products of any other producer, processor, or manufacturer, or to cease doing business with any other person] **to enter into any agreement which is prohibited by Section 8** (e);

(B) **forcing or requiring any person to cease using, selling, handling, transporting, or otherwise dealing in the products of** *any other producer, processor, or manufacturer, or to cease doing business with any other person, or forcing or requiring any other employer to recognize or bargain with a labor organization as the representative of his employees unless such labor organization has been certified as the representative of such employees under the provisions of Section 9 [;]: Provided, That nothing contained in this clause (B) shall be construed to make unlawful, where not otherwise unlawful, any primary strike or primary picketing;*

(C) *forcing or requiring any employer to recognize or bargain with a particular labor organization as the representative of his employees if another labor organization has been certified as the representative of such employees under the provisions of Section 9;*

(D) *forcing or requiring any employer to assign particular work to employees in a particular labor organization or in a particular trade, craft, or class rather than to employees in another labor organization or in another trade, craft, or class, unless such employer is failing to conform to an order or certification of the Board determining the bargaining representative for employees performing such work:*

Provided, That nothing contained in this subsection (b) shall be construed to make unlawful a refusal by any person to enter upon the premises of any employer (other than his own employer), if the employees of such employer are engaged in a strike ratified or approved by a representative of such employees whom such employer is required to recognize under this Act [;]: Provided further, That for the purposes of this paragraph (4) only, nothing contained in such paragraph shall be construed to prohibit publicity, other than picketing, for the purpose of truthfully advising the public, including consumers and members of a labor organization, that a product or products are produced by an employer with whom the labor organization has a primary dispute and are distributed by another employer, as long as such publicity does not have an effect of inducing any individual employed by any person other than the primary employer in the course of his employment to refuse to pick up, deliver, or transport any goods, or not to perform any services, at the establishment of the employer engaged in such distribution;

(5) *to require of employees covered by an agreement authorized under subsection (a) (3) the payment, as a condition precedent to becoming a member of such organization, of a fee in an amount which the Board finds excessive or discriminatory under all the circumstances. In making such a finding, the Board shall consider, among other relevant factors, the practices and customs of labor organizations in the particular industry, and the wages currently paid to the employees affected; [and]*

(6) *to cause or attempt to cause an employer to pay or deliver or agree to pay or deliver any money or other thing of value, in the nature of an exaction, for services which are not performed or not to be performed [.]; and*

(7) *to picket or cause to be picketed, or threaten to picket or cause to be picketed, any employer where an object thereof is forcing or requiring an employer to recognize or bargain with a labor organization as the representative of his employees, or forcing or requiring the employees of an employer to accept or select such labor organization as their collective bargaining representative, unless such labor organization is currently certified as the representative of such employees:*

(A) *where the employer has lawfully recognized in accordance with this Act any other labor organization and a question concerning representation may not appropriately be raised under Section 9 (c) of this Act.*

(B) *where within the preceding twelve months a valid election under Section 9 (c) of this Act has been conducted, or*

(C) *where such picketing has been conducted without a petition under Section 9 (c) being filed within a reasonable period of time not to exceed thirty days from the commencement of such picketing: Provided, That when such a petition has been filed the Board shall forthwith, without regard to the provisions of Section 9 (c) (1) or the absence of a showing of a substantial interest on the part of the labor organization, direct an election in such unit as the Board finds to be appropriate and shall certify the results thereof: Provided further, That nothing in this subparagraph (C) shall be construed to prohibit any picketing or other publicity for the purpose of truthfully advising the public (including consumers) that an employer does not employ members of, or have a contract with, a labor organization, unless an effect of such picketing is to induce any individual employed by any other person in the course of his employment, not to pick up, deliver or transport any goods or not to perform any services.*

Nothing in this paragraph (7) shall be construed to permit any act which would otherwise be an unfair labor practice under this Section 8 (b).

(c) *The expressing of any views, arguments, or opinion, or the dissemination thereof, whether in written, printed, graphic, or visual form, shall not constitute or be evidence of an unfair labor practice under any of the provisions of this Act, if such expression contains no threat of reprisal or force or promise of benefit.*

(d) *For the purpose of this section, to bargain collectively is the performance of the mutual obligation of the employer and the representative of the employees to meet at reasonable times and confer in good faith with respect to wages, hours, and other terms and conditions of employment, or the negotiation of an agreement, or any question arising thereunder, and the execution of a written contract incorporating any agreement reached if requested by either party, but such obligation does not compel either party to agree to a proposal or require the making of a concession: Provided, That where there is in effect a collective-bargaining contract covering employees in an industry affecting commerce, the duty to bargain collectively shall also mean that no party to such contract shall terminate or modify such contract, unless the party desiring such termination or modification—*

(1) *serves a written notice upon the other party to the contract of the proposed termination or modification sixty days prior to the expiration date thereof, or in the event such contract contains no expiration date, sixty days prior to the time it is proposed to make such termination or modification;*

(2) *offers to meet and confer with the other party for the purpose*

of negotiating a new contract or a contract containing the
proposed modifications;

(3) notifies the Federal Mediation and Conciliation Service
within thirty days after such notice of the existence of a dispute, and simultaneously therewith notifies any State or Ter-
ritorial agency established to mediate and conciliate disputes
within the State or Territory where the dispute occurred,
provided no agreement has been reached by that time; and

(4) continues in full force and effect, without resorting to strike
or lockout, all the terms and conditions of the existing contract for a period of sixty days after such notice is given or
until the expiration date of such contract, whichever occurs
later:

The duties imposed upon employers, employees, and labor organizations by paragraphs (2), (3), and (4) shall become inapplicable upon
an intervening certification of the Board, under which the labor organization or individual, which is a party to the contract, has been
superseded as or ceased to be the representative of the employees subject to the provisions of Section 9 (a), and the duties so imposed shall
not be construed as requiring either party to discuss or agree to any
modification of the terms and conditions contained in a contract for a
fixed period, if such modification is to become effective before such
terms and conditions can be reopened under the provisions of the contract. Any employee who engages in a strike within the sixty-day period specified in this subsection shall lose his status as an employee of
the employer engaged in the particular labor dispute, for the purpose
of Sections 8, 9, and 10 of this Act, as amended, but such loss of status
for such employee shall terminate if and when he is reemployed by
such employer.

(e) It shall be an unfair labor practice for any labor organization and any employer to enter into any contract or agreement, express or implied, whereby such employer ceases or
refrains or agrees to cease or refrain from handling, using,
selling, transporting or otherwise dealing in any of the products of any other employer, or to cease doing business with
any other person, and any contract or agreement entered
into heretofore or hereafter containing such an agreement
shall be to such extent unenforcible and void: Provided,

That nothing in this subsection (e) shall apply to an agreement between a labor organization and an employer in the construction industry relating to the contracting or subcontracting of work to be done at the site of the construction, alteration, painting, or repair of a building, structure, or other work: Provided further, That for the purposes of this subsection (e) and Section 8 (b) (4) (B) the terms "any employer," "any person engaged in commerce or an industry affecting commerce," and "any person" when used in relation to the terms "any other producer, processor, or manufacturer," "any other employer," or "any other person" shall not include persons in the relation of a jobber, manufacturer, contractor, or subcontractor working on the goods or premises of the jobber or manufacturer or performing parts of an integrated process or production in the apparel and clothing industry: Provided further, That nothing in this Act shall prohibit the enforcement of any agreement which is within the foregoing exception.

(f) It shall not be an unfair labor practice under subsections (a) and (b) of this section for an employer engaged primarily in the building and construction industry to make an agreement covering employees engaged (or who, upon their employment, will be engaged) in the building and construction industry with a labor organization of which building and construction employees are members (not established, maintained, or assisted by any action defined in Section 8 (a) of this Act as an unfair labor practice) because (1) the majority status of such labor organization has not been established under the provisions of Section 9 of this Act prior to the making of such agreement, or (2) such agreement requires as a condition of employment, membership in such labor organization after the seventh day following the beginning of such employment or the effective date of the agreement, whichever is later, or (3) such agreement requires the employer to notify such labor organization of opportunities for employment with such employer, or gives such labor organization an opportunity to refer qualified applicants for such employment, or (4) such agreement

specifies minimum training or experience qualifications for employment or provides for priority in opportunities for employment based upon length of service with such employer, in the industry or in the particular geographical area: Provided, That nothing in this subsection shall set aside the final proviso to Section 8 (a) (3) of this Act: Provided further, That any agreement which would be invalid, but for clause (1) of this subsection, shall not be a bar to a petition filed pursuant to Section 9 (c) or 9 (e).

Index